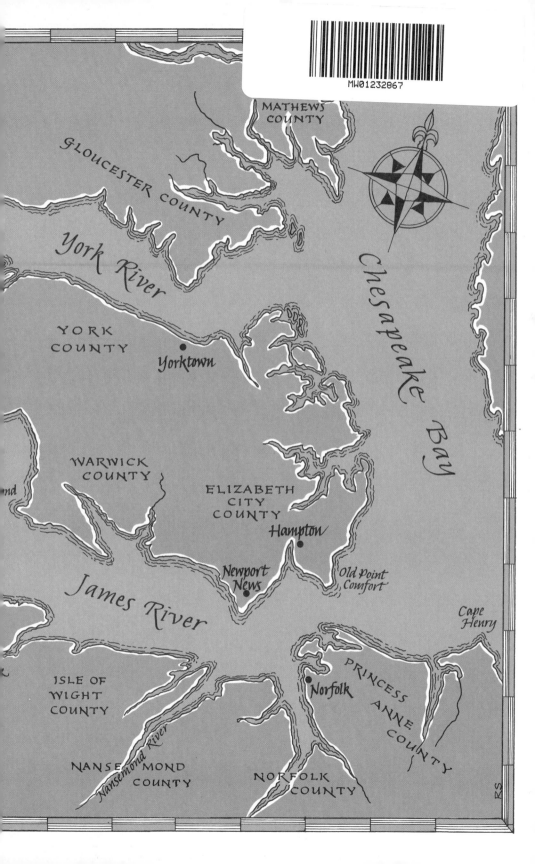

MATHEWS
COUNTY

GLOUCESTER COUNTY

York River

Chesapeake Bay

YORK
COUNTY

Yorktown

WARWICK
COUNTY

nd

ELIZABETH
CITY
COUNTY

Hampton

Newport
News

Old Point
Comfort

James River

Cape
Henry

ISLE OF
WIGHT
COUNTY

PRINCESS
ANNE
COUNTY

Norfolk

NANSEMOND
COUNTY

Nansemond River

NORFOLK
COUNTY

RS

Upper Brandon

Upper Brandon manor house and dependencies viewed from the river side. (prerestoration, 1986)

Upper Brandon

by Robert P. Hilldrup

Published by James River Corporation
Richmond, Virginia

Upper Brandon

*The materials used on the cover are
Imperial Bonded leather L021 Brown Camara and
Skivertex-Antala 2179, made by the James River
Decorative Products Division. The End Leaf is Curtis
Tweedweave basis 80 lb. text, Ivory, and the text, (acid
free) Curtis Brightwater basis 80 lb. text, white, made by
the James River Curtis Mills Division.
Designed by Beatley & Gravitt, Inc.;
Printed by W.M. Brown and Son
and Bound by Nicholstone,
for James River Corporation in 1987.*

The Writing of this Book was Commissioned
by James River Corporation
and the Research was Facilitated
by a Grant from James River Corporation
to the Virginia Historical Society
ISBN 0-9619387-0-6

Prologue

Today visitors approach Upper Brandon much as they did in the nineteenth century and even before—down narrow roads between forests and fields well removed from the main highway that runs generally parallel with the James River on its southern side.

For the plantations that line its banks, though, the river is no longer the highway that it was during much of the history of Upper Brandon. Many ships still ply the James to Richmond, but visitors no longer come by river to Upper Brandon and the other great plantations as they once did.

Thus, despite its proximity to large cities a short distance away by road, Upper Brandon is still largely isolated. It is a quiet place, and when the engines of farm machinery are silent, the sounds of crows cawing in the fields or seabirds calling far out over the James carry easily for a mile or more.

Upper Brandon is a place of rare beauty, where the hand of nature and man projects a harmony, a comfort, and a purpose. It is a land its owners have found easy to love. And it is, equally, a land the visitor finds hard to forget.

Acknowledgements

Most books carry the name of an author; in so doing, they unintentionally mislead the reader because very rarely is any book the result of a single person's imagination, creativity, or effort. That is certainly true of *Upper Brandon*. Although it is not possible to thank or acknowledge everyone who was helpful, that effort certainly needs to be made.

Among the organizations that have contributed to this project are the staff and management of the James River Corporation, the present owners of Upper Brandon; the staffs of the Virginia State Library, the Hopewell *News*, the Petersburg *Progress-Index*, the Prince George County Courthouse, and the Cumberland County Courthouse; and most certainly the Virginia Historical Society, where Mrs. Sally Sartain first suggested the project to me, Dr. Nelson D. Lankford served as editor, and Ms. Joy Weatherley, an undergraduate with the tenacity of an untenured professor, did a professional job of research.

For sharing letters and recollections concerning the plantation, Dr. William Byrd Harrison III, a direct descendant of the builder of Upper Brandon, Mrs. Byrd Davenport, daughter of the last original family owner of Upper Brandon, and Mr. and Mrs. Shirley W. Gray deserve a special word of thanks, as do all those others who somewhere in their lives contributed to the record that has led to this narrative. I wish I could thank you all in person.

Robert P. Hilldrup
Richmond, Virginia
1987

Table of Contents

List of Illustrations

A Note for the Reader

The name *Upper Brandon* did not formally come into existence until the early nineteenth century when the land was divided and the plantation house by that name was built. Before that time, the land was known simply as *Brandon*, a name still properly applied to the plantation house that stands on another portion of the original property a few miles downriver from *Upper Brandon*.

At times, even the residents of *Upper Brandon* referred to their plantation simply as *Brandon*. *Brandon*, in turn, was sometimes known as *Lower Brandon* in an attempt to avoid confusion. In researching and writing this book, every effort has been made to differentiate clearly between the two properties and the two homes. The term *Brandon* is used here in only two ways: (1) when referring to the original property and events before the division of the land, or (2) when, as a point of reference or information, it is necessary to refer to the current house and property of that name.

A Chronology of Events
in the History of Upper Brandon

Upper Brandon Events		**Relevant Historical Events**	
		1607	First permanent English settlement in the New World established at Jamestown, across the James River and 12 miles downstream from Brandon.
John Martin patents the 5,000 acres of Brandon.	1616		
		1620	Pilgrims settle Plymouth.
		1640	Approximate commencement of Colonial style architectural period.
		1676	Bacon's Rebellion.
		1693	College of William and Mary founded.
The Brandon lands are purchased by Benjamin Harrison II, of Wakefield sometime prior to this date.	1712		
		1737	Richmond Founded
		1750	Approximate commencement of Georgian architectural period.
		1765	Approximate construction date of Brandon (Lower) mansion.
		1776	Declaration of Independence.
		1780	Virginia capital moved from Williamsburg to Richmond.
		1781	Americans and French defeat Cornwallis at Yorktown.
		1785	James River Company formed with goal to build Kanawha Canal from Richmond west to the Ohio River.
		1791	Bill of Rights adopted.
		1800	U. S. Census 5,308,000.
Benjamin Harrison III, owner of Brandon, dies. His will divides Brandon between his two sons, George Evelyn Harrison and William Byrd Harrison.	1807	1807	Approximate commencement of Federal architectural period.
		1815	Napoleon defeated at Battle of Waterloo.
		1819	University of Virginia founded by Thomas Jefferson.
		1820	U. S. Census 9,638,000.
		1815	Greek Revival begins to influence U.S. architecture.

Upper Brandon Events		Relevant Historical Events
William Byrd Harrison comes into his inheritance; construction begins on Upper Brandon shortly thereafter.	1821	
Construction of Upper Brandon completed by this year.	1825	
	1826	Thomas Jefferson dies.
William Byrd Harrison marries Mary Randolph Harrison (Polly).	1827	
	1831	Nat Turner leads slave insurrection in Southside Virginia.
	1836	Commence construction of the Louisa Railroad, predecessor of the Chesapeake and Ohio Railroad.
Polly Harrison dies.	1857	
William Byrd Harrison marries Ellen Wayles Randolph. Wings on central Upper Brandon mansion constructed.	1859	
William Byrd Harrison sends four sons to the army of the Confederate States of America. His eldest, Benjamin, is killed in 1862 at Malvern Hill.	1861	1861 The Civil War begins.
	1863	Emancipation Proclamation.
	1865	End of Civil War.
William Byrd Harrison dies. Upper Brandon is left to two of his sons.	1870	
Upper Brandon purchased by George Harrison Byrd, William Byrd Harrison's nephew.	1871	
Randolph Harrison dies, the last of William Byrd Harrison's sons by his first marriage.	1900	
	1945	World War II Ends.
Upper Brandon passes from the hands of the last Harrison descendant, Francis Otway Byrd. Purchased by Harry C. Thompson of Hopewell.	1948	
Upper Brandon purchased by Curles Neck Farms. Mansion ceases to be occupied.	1961	
	1969	James River Corporation Founded
Upper Brandon purchased by James River Corporation.	1984	

Upper Brandon

CHAPTER ONE

Origins

The land of Upper Brandon lies on the southern shore of the James River in Prince George County, Virginia, some twelve miles above the site of Jamestown, the first permanent English settlement in the New World. It lies about thirty miles downstream, if one disregards the twists and turns in the James, from the city of Richmond.

Long before the arrival of man and the building of his cities and plantations, however, a geologic trauma fixed the landscape of this part of eastern America. That event set the rock-strewn falls across the great tidal rivers and thus separated the Piedmont from the coastal plain, or the Tidewater.

Because of this event, when man first began his travels up these great rivers, he found that the river falls blocked the passage of his boats. At such points he had to change his mode of transportation. There, where Piedmont and Tidewater met, villages, towns, and cities began to grow—Alexandria on the Potomac, Fredericksburg on the Rappahannock, Petersburg on the Appomattox, Raleigh on the Neuse, Augusta on the Savannah, and Richmond on the James.

This geologic event also ensured something else. It turned each of these rivers below their falls into tidal waters, meandering in loops and coils, and, as carriers of nutrients from the mountains and hills, into creators of rich and fertile farmland along their shores. Such was the event that created the peninsula of some 5,000 acres that became Brandon plantation and that, in due time, was divided into Brandon and Upper Brandon, a home and heritage to many families, but particularly to the Harrisons.

It is difficult to say with certainty when men first came to the land of Upper Brandon. One study conducted in 1985, shortly after the James River Corporation purchased the Upper Brandon property, uncovered projectile points indicating habitation from the Archaic or Early Woodland

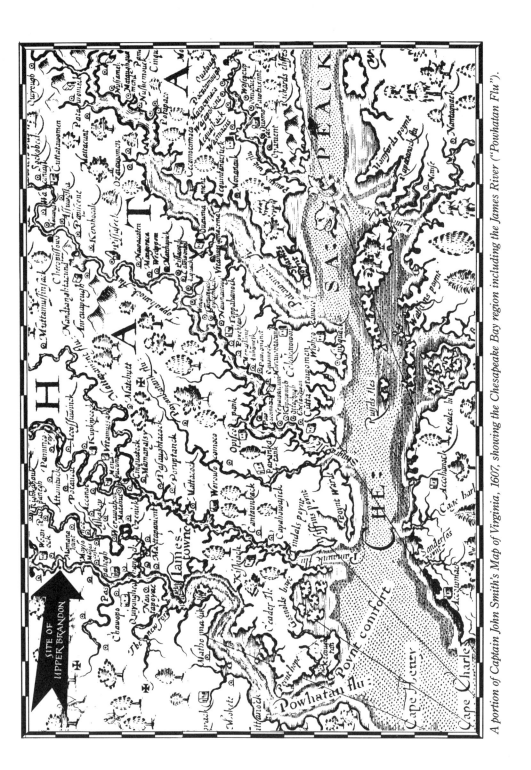

A portion of Captain John Smith's Map of Virginia, 1607, showing the Chesapeake Bay region including the James River ("Powhatan Flu").

Periods (8,000 BC-1,000 BC). The study also produced evidence in the form of pottery that showed "extensive prehistoric settlement" on the bottomlands between Kennon Marsh and the James River, a site just downstream from the mansion. The pottery dates from the Middle and Late Woodland Periods (500 BC to AD 1607).[1]

The same study also discovered the remains of a small, early colonial site dating to about 1640, where bits of pottery, English pipe stem fragments, flint, and glass were collected.[2] The dating of the site is particularly important, for it represents an English presence close to the time of the first white owner of the plantation. That man was the volatile and enigmatic John Martin, one of the founders of Jamestown and a man whose life was marked with strife and controversy. Martin, it is said in one assessment of his life, was "contentious, obstreperous and contumacious."[3] It was an assessment that his life surely bore out.

Of John Martin, we know both a great deal and very little. Parts of his life are well recorded and others are left in shadow. We know, for example, that he usually saw or projected himself in one way and that his enemies, who consisted at one time or another of most of the people he knew, generally perceived him in another.

John Martin was a leader; of that we can be certain. An accomplished mariner who had sailed with Sir Francis Drake, he was one of seven men, including Captains John Smith and Christopher Newport, named to the Council of the Virginia Company at Jamestown early in 1607. As master of ordnance, Martin was responsible for building the original James Fort. Although relations with the natives foundered almost immediately upon the arrival of the English, he managed to complete his task quickly and in spite of at least two Indian attacks.[4]

---

1. Nicholas Luccketti, senior historical archaeologist, Virginia Department of Conservation and Historic Resources, Division of Historic Landmarks, to Brenton Halsey, chairman and chief executive officer, James River Corporation, April 8, 1985.
2. Ibid.
3. Martha Woodroof Hiden, "Virginia County Records: Their Background and Scope," *Virginia Magazine of History and Biography* (hereafter cited as *VMHB*), LIV (1946), 22.
4. Samuel M. Bemiss, "John Martin of Brandon," in *An Address before the Jamestown Society [at] Richmond, Virginia, November 9, 1963*, pp. 6, 8.

In July of 1607, however, the "summer sickness" devastated the little settlement. Whether the malady was typhoid, or malaria, or some other disease is not known, but the results were disastrous. The sickness left Martin weak in body and depressed in spirit, for his son, a youth of fourteen, did not survive the epidemic.[5]

The hardships of the Jamestown colony came close to destroying this latest attempt by Englishmen to establish a permanent foothold in the New World. Only thirty-eight of those who arrived in 1607 survived the winter. The winter of 1609-10 was even worse. Of the 490 people in the colony in October 1609, including many newcomers, only about sixty were alive six months later. Yet it was here that the mettle of the man who founded Brandon was tested—"all save John Martin voted to abandon the Colony."[6] His powers of persuasion, when he wished to use them, must have been significant.

During these early, harsh years of the colony, Martin looked south across the James. He may have begun cultivation of land there as early as 1611. By the time he received his patent for 5,000 acres in 1616, he had already attempted to cultivate silk, tobacco, fruit, and vegetables. When he sailed that year for London in the ship *Treasurer*, he was accompanied by the spoils of land and water (which included sassafras, pitch, sturgeon, and caviar) and by the Indian princess Pocahontas, John Rolfe, and their young son.[7]

The patent that Martin received in London was not the solution to his troubles that he might have expected. At that time, a patent was an award or grant, frequently of land, given by the king in return for services rendered.[8] It proved an ideal way to spur interest in colonizing a new land. Martin's patent covered 10 shares at 500 acres per share and caused controversy for most of the remainder of Martin's life. This strife resulted because the patent, at the behest of James I, gave Martin "sundry extra privileges," despite "the dislike of divers of the commit-

5. Ibid.
6. Ibid., p. 10. There is some disagreement among the sources about the exact numbers of survivors. See Richard L. Morton, *Colonial Virginia*, Vol. 1: *The Tidewater Period, 1607-1710* (Chapel Hill, 1960), pp. 13-27.
7. Bemiss, "John Martin of Brandon," p. 11.
8. *Black's Law Dictionary* (3d ed.; St. Paul, Minn., 1933), p. 1336.

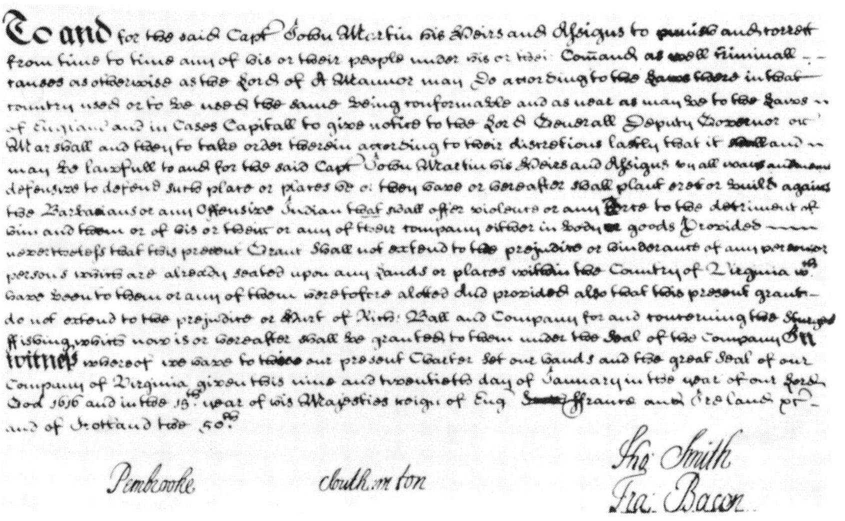
Pembrooke
Southampton
Tho: Smith
Fra: Bacon

The closing portion of the original 1616 patent granted to "Capt. John Martin Esq." by "The Company of Virginia" with the "consent of His Majesties Counsel of Virginia" for the land that became Brandon. Considerable controversy was provoked among Martin's fellow colonists by the provision which gave Martin the right "to govern and comand" his people "free from any comand of the Colony—". It is interesting to note that one signer of this original patent was the well-known English philosopher and statesman Francis Bacon (1561-1626).

tee" responsible for carrying out the king's wishes.[9] It was at this time that the land acquired the name that it still bears—the family name of Martin's wife, Mary, the daughter of Sir Richard Brandon.[10]

Although Martin's reputation for being bold and abrasive was already established, his sojourn in England in 1616-17 further set him at odds with many of his fellow colonists. For what brought the most problems was a series of provisos in his patent stating, for example, that Martin would "to all Intents & Purposes [be entitled] as any Lord of any Mannor here in England Doth Hold his lands." The provision that irritated his fellow colonists most granted Martin, his heirs, executors, and assigns, the right "to govern and comand all such persons . . . *free from any comand of the Colony* [author's emphasis] except it be in aiding and assisting the same against Foreign or Domesticall Enemy."[11]

---

9. "The Case of Captain Martin," in "Sainsbury's Abstracts," *VMHB*, VII (1900), 269.
10. Bemiss, "John Martin of Brandon," p. 11.
11. John Martin's patent, Virginia State Library, Richmond (hereafter cited as VSL).

Within seven years the quarrels and complaints about Martin's privileges had become so extensive that he was forced to accept a new patent that restricted his rights, but not his property.[12] Martin's troubles were still not over, however. Some evidence suggests that he was cast into debtor's prison while in London and from there issued a pitiful plea to the king for aid, citing a fire that had destroyed all his houses in Virginia with a loss of some 2,000 pounds sterling. The plea was replete with examples of what Martin perceived as the treachery and abuse he had received from his associates.[13]

Martin's life (ca.1562-ca.1632) stretched from the reign of Queen Elizabeth I to that of Charles I, a period in which boldness was clearly an asset to the expansion of an England destined for empire. Martin saw potential all around him. On a visit to the Indian chief Powhatan in 1614, for example, at a time when physical safety was a primary concern for most colonists, he became absorbed in studying the plants the Indians grew with an obvious eye to commerce and to the benefit of John Martin.[14]

Such was the man that he could be labeled "troublesome at sea," as noted following his voyage back to the New World in 1609, apparently because whoever was in charge was not willing to do things his way.[15] Indeed, in 1635, three years after Martin's reported death, Richard Kemp, the secretary of Virginia, was called upon by the Lords Commissioners for Plantations to give "a true and perfect relation of the late distempers here, caused by Capt. Martin."[16]

Even in old age, Martin remained tough. He was a "gentleman pirate" who loved controversy, yet his accomplishments for his colony and his plantation were impressive.[17] Martin died about 1632. Some accounts

------

12. Hiden, "Virginia County Records," p. 56.
13. Ibid., pp. 62-63.
14. Ibid., p. 39.
15. Matthew Page Andrews, *The Soul of a Nation: The Founding of Virginia and the Projection of New England* (New York, 1944), p. 148.
16. W. Noël Sainsbury, ed., *Calendar of State Papers, Colonial Series, 1574-1660...* (London, 1860), p. 207.
17. Ibid., p. 63; Bemiss, "John Martin of Brandon," p. 12.

say his body was buried in a grave, now lost, at Brandon.[18] Others suggest that he never returned from England to see his beloved plantation again.[19] Whatever the place of John Martin's death, his estate passed to a grandson, Robert Bargrave, probably the issue of a daughter from a later marriage, because Martin's only son had died at Jamestown.[20]

The saga of John Martin and the founding of Brandon is a colorful one. Martin's strength of body and belief was surely necessary in the taming of a wild new land, and it is doubtful that a lesser man could have done as much, faced as he was with opposition, both real and imagined, from his own people in America and in England.

18. Ibid.
19. Hiden, "Virginia County Records," p. 63.
20. Bemiss, "John Martin of Brandon," p. 12.

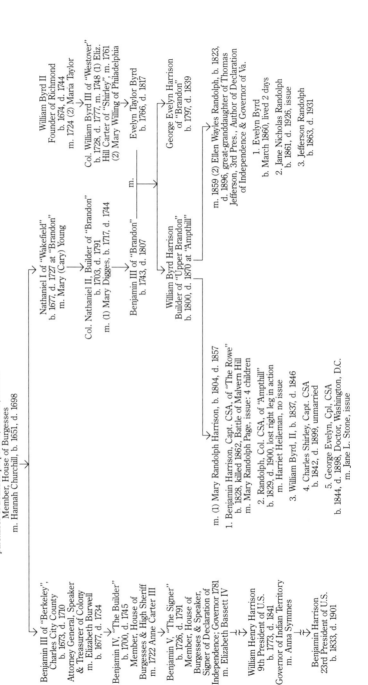

Benjamin Harrison I
Emigrant—c. 1632, d. 1646, Jamestown
Member, House of Burgesses 1642
m. Mary

Benjamin Harrison II, of "Wakefield", Surry County,
purchaser of Brandon properties, b. 1645, d. 1712
Member, House of Burgesses
m. Hannah Churchill, b. 1651, d. 1698

William Byrd II
Founder of Richmond
b. 1674, d. 1744
m. 1724 (2) Maria Taylor

Col. William Byrd III of "Westover"
b. 1728, d. 1777, m. 1748 (1) Eliz.
Hill Carter of "Shirley", m. 1761
(2) Mary Willing of Philadelphia

Evelyn Taylor Byrd
b. 1766, d. 1817

Nathaniel I of "Wakefield"
b. 1677, d. 1727 at "Brandon"
m. Mary (Cary) Young

Col. Nathaniel II, Builder of "Brandon"
b. 1703, d. 1791
m. (1) Mary Digges, b. 1717, d. 1744

Benjamin III of "Brandon"
b. 1743, d. 1807

William Byrd Harrison
Builder of "Upper Brandon"
b. 1800, d. 1870 at "Ampthill"

George Evelyn Harrison
of "Brandon"
b. 1797, d. 1839

m.

m. 1859 (2) Ellen Wayles Randolph, b. 1823,
d. 1896, great-granddaughter of Thomas
Jefferson, 3rd Pres., Author of Declaration
of Independence & Governor of Va.

1. Evelyn Byrd
b. March 1860, lived 2 days

2. Jane Nicholas Randolph
b. 1861, d. 1926, issue

3. Jefferson Randolph
b. 1863, d. 1931

Benjamin III of "Berkeley",
Charles City County
Attorney General, Speaker
& Treasurer of Colony
m. Elizabeth Burwell
b. 1677, d. 1734

Benjamin IV, "The Builder"
b. 1700, d. 1745
Member, House of
Burgesses & High Sheriff
m. 1722 Anne Carter III

Benjamin V, "The Signer"
b. 1726, d. 1791
Member, House of
Burgesses & Speaker,
Signer of Declaration of
Independence; Governor 1781
m. Elizabeth Bassett IV

William Henry Harrison
9th President of U.S.
b. 1773, d. 1841
Governor of Indian Territory
m. Anna Symmes

Benjamin Harrison
23rd President of U.S.
b. 1833, d. 1901

m. (1) Mary Randolph Harrison, b. 1804, d. 1857

1. Benjamin Harrison, Capt. CSA, of "The Rowe"
b. 1828, killed 1862, Battle of Malvern Hill
m. Mary Randolph Page, issue: 4 children

2. Randolph, Col. CSA, of "Ampthill"
b. 1829, d. 1900, lost right leg in action
m. Harriet Heileman, no issue

3. William Byrd, II, b. 1837, d. 1846

4. Charles Shirley, Capt. CSA
b. 1842, d. 1899, unmarried

5. George Evelyn, Cpl. CSA
b. 1844, d. 1898, Doctor, Washington, D.C.
m. Jane L. Stone, issue

Harrison Genealogy Relating to Upper Brandon.

CHAPTER TWO

Harrison Legacy

In the years that passed between the death of John Martin and the division of the Brandon lands that led to the creation of Upper Brandon, the property passed through various hands. Richard Quiney, a native of Stratford-on-Avon, purchased the property from John Martin's grandson and shared ownership of Brandon with John Sadler and possibly with William Barker (or Barber).[1] For almost one hundred years, these men or their heirs were absentee owners.[2]

Quiney also appears to have been joint owner with John Sadler not only of the Brandon plantation, still known at this time as Martin's Brandon, but also of nearby Merchant's Hope plantation. Quiney, "citizen and grocer" of London, died in 1655 and left all his Virginia lands, as well as his servants and cattle there, to his son, Thomas. The Brandon property appears to have increased in size since Martin's day, for by the time it passed into Harrison hands it contained 7,000 acres, 2,000 more than the original plantation.[3]

It was sometime prior to 1712 when the land came into the possession of the Harrisons, and thereby began a period of family ownership that lasted over two centuries and was associated with the property's primary development as well as the construction of the plantation house of Upper Brandon. The purchaser apparently was Benjamin Harrison II, who in his will dated April 16, 1711 left "all my land in Martin's Brandon in Prince George County" to his son Nathaniel Harrison (1677-1727), of Wakefield, in Surry County.[4] This is supported by the information that Nathaniel's parents, who died in 1698 and 1712, are said

1. Quiney was the son-in-law of William Shakespeare. W. G. Stanard, "Abstracts of Virginia Land Patents," *VMHB*, IV (1897), 315.
2. "The Indians of Southern Virginia, 1650-1711," ibid., VII (1899-1900), 357, n. 9
3. Stanard, "Abstracts of Virginia Land Patents," p. 315.
4. W. Gordon Harrison, Jr. to Brenton S. Halsey, May 28, 1987.

by at least one source to be buried in the Harrison family cemetery at Brandon.[5]

The Harrison line in Virginia and other parts of America is a distinguished one, numbering among its branches a signer of the Declaration of Independence, Benjamin Harrison (the "Signer"); two presidents of the United States, William Henry Harrison (1773-1841) and Benjamin Harrison (1833-1901).

Numerous other Harrisons served as public officials, including many who were members of the Virginia House of Burgesses (later the House of Delegates), the oldest legislative body in the Western hemisphere. Through marriage, the Harrisons were linked to other equally distinguished families, particularly the Lees of both Revolutionary War and Civil War fame, and to William Byrd, the founder of Richmond.

The root of the Harrison family in America was Benjamin Harrison, who came to Virginia sometime before 1632 and died at Jamestown in

*Benjamin Harrison of Brandon
(1743-1807), father of
William Byrd Harrison,
by Saint-Memin.*

1646. He was a member of the House of Burgesses and left one son, Chancellor Benjamin Harrison II, of Wakefield in Surry, the county lying immediately below Prince George County on the southern shore of the James River.[6]

Benjamin Harrison II, who also served in the House of Burgesses, was born in 1645 and died in 1712. He and his wife, Hannah Churchill Harrison (1651-1698), were the parents of five children, including Nathaniel, who married Mrs. Mary Young, the daughter of John Cary, and was the father of seven children. Among

---

5. "Upper Brandon: Architectural Notes and Comments", also, verified by examination of the gravestones at Brandon family cemetery.

6. The information on the Harrison family through the sixth generation, and on the formal division of the lands that created Upper Brandon plantation, is taken from an extensive genealogical tree prepared by Kate Duval Harrison in 1934 (Virginia Historical Society, Richmond [hereafter cited as VHS]). Although some errors appear in it, the information about the early Harrisons before the founding of Upper Brandon appears correct when compared with other accounts.

those children was Colonel Nathaniel Harrison, who in 1765 built the Brandon plantation house.

Colonel Harrison married twice. His second marriage, from which there was no issue, was to Mrs. Lucy Carter Fitzhugh, daughter of Robert "King" Carter, renowned for his lands and homes in Virginia's Northern Neck, between the Rappahannock and Potomac Rivers. The first marriage, however, produced yet another Benjamin Harrison (1743-1807), who in turn married three times with only the third marriage producing issue. That marriage was to Evelyn Taylor Byrd of Westover, the home of the founder of Richmond, William Byrd, and one of several great plantations across the river and just upstream from Brandon. Among their children—the sixth generation of Virginia Harrisons—were George Evelyn Harrison (1797-1839) and William Byrd Harrison (1800-1870), the builder of Upper Brandon.

Upon his death in 1807, Benjamin Harrison, or Benjamin III as he is sometimes known to avoid confusion with his ancestors and other relatives of the same name, left his lands, the original Brandon plantation, to his two sons, George and William.[7] He also provided from other portions of his estate for his daughters, Ann and Elizabeth. Elizabeth, also known as Lizzie, married Alfred Powell. Ann also known as Nanny or Nannie, married Richard Evelyn Byrd, of Winchester, great grandfather of polar explorer Admiral Richard E. Byrd and of Virginia Governor and U.S. Senator Harry F. Byrd.

The division of the 7,000 acres between the two sons gave 3,550 acres to William Byrd Harrison for what became Upper Brandon.[8] The will of Benjamin III apparently provided that each of the sons would receive his property at the age of twenty-one.[9] The will thus gave George Evelyn Harrison the plantation house at Brandon and a three-year head start on his younger brother as well. Nothing comparable to Brandon

---

7. Will of Benjamin Harrison, 1807; as cited in Elizabeth Temple Johnston McRee comp., "Upper Brandon: "Chronological and Genealogical History" p. 4; see also Ann Harrison's signed receipt for her father's legacy, executed at Richmond, February 5, 1824, Harrison Family Papers, VHS.
8. McRee, comp., "Upper Brandon: Chronological and Genealogical History," p. 4.
9. Ibid. See also land tax records for Prince George County, archives division.

William Byrd Harrison (1800-1870), builder of Upper Brandon. This oil portrait was painted in 1835 by the noted English born artist, William James Hubard (1807-1862). In a letter dated May 9, 1835 Mr. Harrison's sister Elizabeth Page Harrison Powell noted "Mr. Hubard is coming on slowly with his pictures, but seems to be highly thought of as a painter. Our brothers wrote on form Mr. Sully, but have declined employing him, he has increased his charges and for a likeness without hand he charged $150, for a head $100, and for half size (like Miss Blounts) $400, & for a full length likeness $800, did you ever hear of such charges in our Country—".

would be built on the Upper Brandon property for almost twenty years after the death of Benjamin III.[10]

In the years just before reaching his majority, William Byrd Harrison left home to attend college. Like many other young Virginia gentlemen in this period, he looked north, to Harvard, rather than to the College of William and Mary, located just across the river in Williamsburg. Why young William chose Harvard, or who might have made the choice for him, is not known.[11] Perhaps, as his later letters showed, it was simply an early manifestation of a desire for travel. In any event, a letter to his sister Ann, who was the object of most of the surviving correspondence either brother produced, provides a light-hearted commentary. Writing from Cambridge on May 16, 1819, he said, "I have, for the last week, been constantly intending to occupy my first leisure moments in the pleasing task of writing to your ladyship; but the execution of this *grand* design has been delayed until the present time."[12]

Despite his spritely tone, however, William hinted at a sense of homesickness in that unfamiliar northern environment. He spoke of longing to see a new nephew and, because it was springtime and the planting season had begun, observed, "I suppose, by this time, this generous earth is beginning to bestow its fruit, with bounteous hand, on our happy southern people. The contrast between this country...is extremely great...I do not admire their houses very much, as they prefer wood to stone in their construction."[13] When the time came to construct Upper Brandon, Harrison followed this sentiment and the example of many other owners of plantation houses in Virginia—he eschewed the bountiful supply of wood in the vast forest nearby and chose instead to build of brick.

---

10. Petersburg *Intelligencer*, August 11, 1807.
11. In Richard A. May's "Harvard and Virginia" (Harvard Club of Virginia, 1958), "William B. Harrison, Petersburg," is listed as a recipient of a bachelor's degree in 1820. Harrison's graduation certificate is in the possession of William B. Harrison III, of Richmond, a professor at Virginia Commonwealth University. According to May, sixty-nine Virginians enrolled at Harvard between 1800 and 1860 "for the basic classical higher education not obtainable at home." Many well-known Virginia names are on May's list.
12. William B. Harrison to Ann H. Byrd, May 16, 1819, Byrd Family Paper, VHS.
13. Ibid.

View from the land side with the James River flowing left to right in the background. As it stands today, Upper Brandon represents two phases of construction: the main building, together with the two dependencies and connecting hyphens, all completed about 1825, and two wings added to the main structure thirty-four years later, in 1859.

CHAPTER THREE

The Mansion

William Byrd Harrison formally came into his inheritance in 1821, when he reached his majority and began almost at once to plan a plantation house that would rival his brother's home a few miles away. Just who designed Upper Brandon is not known.[1] Like most great homes of the period, it faces the water, because the great rivers of America were the primary avenues of travel and commerce in the eighteenth and nineteenth centuries.[2]

The site on which Upper Brandon stands is just upstream from the point at which the James River turns from its generally southeastern course in a sharp southerly bend around a peninsula known as Kennon Marsh. Visitors today are impressed not only by the house itself but also by the remains of the large serpentine boxwood garden that stand next to the building on the upstream side. Because the only other such garden of that period in Virginia is at Monticello, some observers speculate that Jefferson influenced the landscaping at Upper Brandon.[3] Although many of the trees that adorned Upper Brandon have been lost to time and the elements, some grand examples remain, particularly willow oaks and tulip poplars over one hundred feet tall. A sketch made in 1931 shows that the grounds immediately next to the

---

1. Edward A. Wyatt IV, *Plantation Houses Around Petersburg: In the Counties of Prince George, Chesterfield and Dinwiddie, Virginia* (Petersburg, 1955), p. 4.
2. Although there is no record of any other home on the site where Upper Brandon now stands, the size of the magnolias and the English boxwood "suggest a theory that the grounds may have been beautified for the purpose well before construction was begun" (Ibid).
3. William M. Kelso, historical archaeologist, to Richard C. Erickson, James River Corporation, October 22, 1985. Evidence for the Jefferson connection is shaky and rests on the fact that the gardens at Upper Brandon and Monticello are similar and the fact that William Byrd Harrison's second wife was a great granddaughter of Jefferson, Ellen Wayles Randolph. Harrison did not marry her, however, until just before the Civil War. Thus the Jefferson influence is tenuous.

This photo, circa 1870, shows a parapet, assumed to be original, which was derived from Asher Benjamin's, American Builder's Companion, *a popular pattern book used by craftsmen of the early 19th century.*

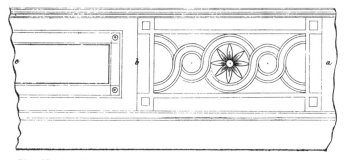

Plate Number 53
Following Page Number 102

house contained pecans, hackberries, elms, oaks, hollies, magnolias, poplars, beeches, ash, red cedar, sweet gum, and locust.[4]

As it stands today, Upper Brandon represents two phases of construction: the main building, together with the two dependencies and connecting hyphens, all completed about 1825, and two wings added to the main structure thirty-four years later, in 1859. A present-day review describes the architectural style of the house as "Federal-Neo-Classical but somewhat restrained."[5] This account also points out that the land-side porch roof is supported with Ionic columns while the river side has Composite order columns. Another account describes Upper Brandon as "one of the...most architecturally correct Virginia houses" of Federal style.[6] Excluding the dependencies, the building consists of a full basement, first floor, second floor, and attic. Each floor is 3,756 square feet. Basement passages, or hyphens, connect the two-story dependencies with the main house.[7]

The floor plan of the original house is characterized by the front and back first-floor porticoes and the balance that the dependencies give on either end. The first floor of the west dependency housed the kitchen and laundry. Food was delivered by the servants through the underground hyphen. The east dependency is thought to have been a school or office, and access through the east hyphen was never completed. Facing the home with the river at one's back, the familiar Palladian plan common to eighteenth-century Tidewater plantations is apparent. The first floor of the main building contains an entrance hall running the full depth of the house, twin parlors on the east side, and a dining room and nursery on the west. On the second floor was another full-depth hall with two large bedrooms on either side.

The interior of Upper Brandon seems ornate even to the eye of the casual visitor. The woodwork is particularly notable, created by craftsmen competent in executing neoclassical styles. The use of pattern

4. "Measured Plan of Upper Brandon, Prince George County, Virginia, June, 1931."
5. G. Alan Morledge, AIA, "Architectural Inspection of Upper Brandon," September 8, 1984, pp. 1-20.
6. Edith Tunis Sale, "Upper Brandon: The James River Home of Mr. and Mrs. Francis Otway Byrd," from an unknown serial, ca. 1930, p. 50.
7. Gordon B. Galusha, "Architectural Report, Upper Brandon Plantation," June 7, 1985, p. 1.

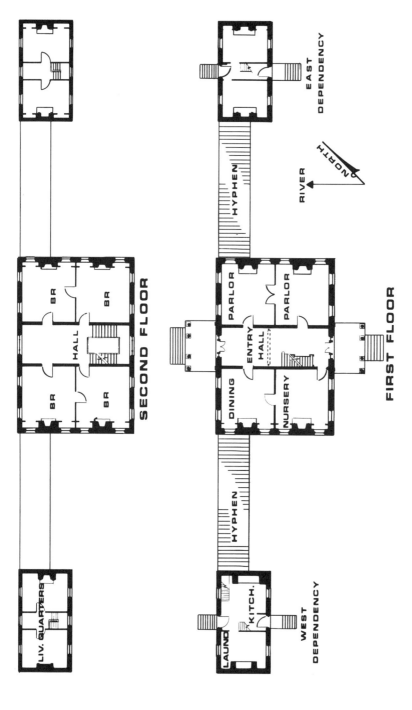

SECOND FLOOR

LIV. QUARTERS

BR

BR

HALL

BR

BR

FIRST FLOOR

EAST
DEPENDENCY

NORTH

RIVER

HYPHEN

PARLOR

PARLOR

ENTRY
HALL

DINING

NURSERY

HYPHEN

LAUND.

KITCH.

WEST
DEPENDENCY

Original plans for the house have not been found, but this representation of the floor plan is believed to be essentially correct based on information derived from the surviving structure and from written references. History of specific room use varies some by account, for instance the east dependency is mentioned both as a school house and an office and indeed it may have served both uses at different times.

books was common during the period, and it is interesting to note that exact drawings of many of the details in the plantation house appear in Asher Benjamin's *American Builder's Companion,*[8] published prior to the construction of Upper Brandon. Graceful curves and arches mark the doorways from room to room. Molding is elaborate and care-

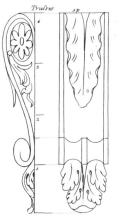

Entry Hall
Door Molding

Plate Number 33
Following Page Number 70

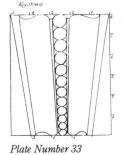

Keystone of
Entry Hall Arch

Plate Number 33
Following Page Number 70

These photographs from Upper Brandon provide additional evidence that the craftsmen building the Manor House used Boston architect Asher Benjamin's pattern book.

8. Asher Benjamin, *American Builder's Companion,* 1806 (revised through 6 editions till 1827).

fully detailed. An arch embellished with carving and carried on fluted pilasters with Ionic capitals spans the broad center hall. A gouged chair rail encircles the hall, while acanthus-leaf carving surmounts the four inner doors, on which one finds crosses instead of the customary rectangles.[9]

An inspection of the main house shows that Harrison used Flemish bond pattern and a rather large brick, but that either the original molds were lost or Harrison changed his mind when the dependencies were constructed, for a somewhat smaller brick was used there.[10] A "widow's walk" or "captain's walk" overlooks the river from the second story. A circa 1870 photo of Upper Brandon shows a parapet, presumed to be original, which was also derived from Benjamin's pattern book. It gave the manor house a sophisticated horizontal Regency appearance unlike most Virginia plantation homes.

Upper Brandon is clearly related to three contemporary Virginia Houses: Hampstead (New Kent Co.), Horn Quarter (King William Co.) and Magnolia Grange (Chesterfield Co.). The woodwork in all four houses is so similar, it is probable that it was executed by the same craftsmen. Also, the exterior facade of Upper Brandon is so close to that of the Governor's Mansion and the Wickham-Valentine House in Richmond, both by Alexander Parris of Boston, it can be speculated that the same builder may have been involved with each.

The covered passages from the west dependency to the main house provided access between the kitchen and the main house. This is a style common to a number of Virginia houses of similar quality—for example, Mount Airy in Richmond County and Blandfield in Essex County.[11] The reason for the separation, of course, is simple: the danger of fire to the main building was reduced and the clutter of cooking and the presence of slaves or servants was controlled.

The attic of the main house was never finished and remains in nearly original condition. The location of the collar beams, seven feet above the floor, suggests that Harrison may have been considering the addition of dormer windows and another level of living quarters. The

9. Sale, "Upper Brandon," p. 50.
10. Morledge, "Architectural Inspection," pp. 1-2.
11. Calder Loth to Brenton S. Halsey, May 11, 1987, James River Corporation of Virginia.

View of East parlor on the riverside looking into the library during Francis Otway Byrd's ownership, circa 1940.

View of the same parlor, in an obvious state of disrepair. Date of this photo is not known.

A circa 1880 photo of some of Upper Brandon's out-buildings, a farm overseer's house on the left, and slave quarters on the right. The sacks of grain are headed to the dock for shipment as can be seen by referring to the picture on page 46, apparently taken later the same day. The overseer's house remains today and is being restored by James River Corporation to house the plantation manager's offices.

presence of a finished stairway that runs from the second floor to the attic directly above the main stairway supports this theory.[12]

By 1859, when the wings were being built, bathrooms with indoor water closets were already fashionable as a replacement for chamber pots. Details of this remodeling were mentioned in a letter to James E. Gray, a local contractor, which discussed the placement of soil lines and routing.[13]

Other correspondence from this period reveals that both Harrison and his wife took an active interest in the new construction and in renovations and repairs to the plantation house. An example of this attention to detail is found in a letter to Gray from Mrs. Harrison in which she suggests that "the pins [be] taken out of the pillars in the Hall, before the wood work is painted, and also that the domed glass over the mantle in the room over the nursery, and the looking glass in the room over the Parlor shall be taken down before the rooms are painted." She also warned that woodwork on a stairway in her dressing room and two other rooms must be varnished, not painted, nor should the plated knobs for the downstairs doorway nor the brown ones "for the rooms above" be neglected.[14]

An undated list suggests that gay and lively colors were part of either the redecorating of Upper Brandon or the work on the wings. The handwritten list, entitled "Callor [sic] of W. B. Harrison House," lists such items as "crome yellars in oil, Parrish Green, Burnt Umbers in oil, crome Green, Lamp Black," and various blue and whites.[15] Another example of Harrison's attention to detail reads, "The ceiling all dead white. The walls very light in no case at all darker than the samples sent."[16]

In addition to the building, expansion, and renovation of the main house at Upper Brandon, many other service buildings were necessary

---

12. Morledge, pp. 6-7.
13. George Bargamin, Jr., to James E. Gray, Nov. 1859, original in possession of Mr. and Mrs. Shirley W. Gray of Burrowsville. Mr. Gray is the grandson of James E. Gray.
14. Ellen Wayles Randolph Harrison to James Gray, November 7, 1859, original in possession of Mr. and Mrs. Shirley W. Gray.
15. List, original in possession of Mr. and Mrs. Shirley W. Gray.
16. Undated note labeled "for the painter" in possession of Mr. and Mrs. Shirley W. Gray.

for William Byrd Harrison to establish a working plantation. Various outbuildings for farm implements, as well as pens for animals were required. An ice house, the remains of which still stand just downriver from the mansion, was a requirement for the chilling and preservation of foods and beverages. Living quarters for slaves were also constructed on the property.

An example of one of these auxiliary buildings is found in a bill for timber to construct a stable forty-four feet wide and one hundred feet long.[17] Because stables normally contain a second story where hay and other food for animals are kept in proximity to livestock and safe from the weather, these dimensions would have created a building of almost 9,000 square feet. The bill mentions 300 birch studs 3" x 4" and eighteen feet in length; 60 rafters each thirty feet long; in all, 33 lots of wood, exclusive of shingles, and including 8 massive beams forty-seven feet in length.[18] This stable, unfortunately, no longer exists, and nothing apparently is known of its demise.

During the period of construction and renovation, from the early 1820s to the eve of the Civil War, Upper Brandon was a prime example of a flourishing Virginia plantation, as correspondence from family members and visitors reveals. With the plantation house as its focal point, Upper Brandon was the scene of happiness and sorrow, of conformity to the mores of time and place, and of agricultural innovation that set it apart from most of the farms of the era. The house bears witness not only to the care and attention to detail that went into its construction but also to the sense of place, family, and purpose that motivated the young William Byrd Harrison when he made the decision to build. Although there was no lack of affection between him and his elder brother, William decided that he, too, would have a home on his share of the old family lands, one that would rival his brother George's inheritance of Brandon. Many who visit both homes today believe that he succeeded.

---

17. The bill is the property of Mr. and Mrs. Shirley W. Gray, who relate that it was for construction at Upper Brandon. Unfortunately, the bill is not dated, nor are there any financial figures to indicate what all this lumber cost or if it was milled from timber on the Harrison property.
18. A bill in the possession of Mr. and Mrs. Shirley W. Gray.

CHAPTER FOUR

Plantation Social Life and Health

The building of Upper Brandon was probably completed in 1825, the year that Prince George County tax records show an increase in the assessed value on the property from a few hundred dollars to $7,000. Soon afterwards William Byrd Harrison had occasion to visit another plantation, Clifton, in Cumberland County about forty miles west of Richmond.

The object of his attention was a fourth cousin, Mary Randolph Harrison, the daughter of Randolph Harrison and another Mary Randolph Harrison.[1] Thus, William took as his betrothed a woman who already bore his last name and whose full name was the same as her mother's (who, in turn, bore a maiden name the same as her husband's first name). Unraveling the mysteries of Virginia genealogy is not a task for the unwary. Fortunately, somewhere along the way the bride-to-be acquired the nickname "Polly," and it was in that manner that she was addressed by family and friends throughout her life.

Preparations for the marriage immersed the bride's parents in the details of planning an important social event in the life of their family and their plantation. Writing from Richmond, Randolph Harrison confessed to his wife that "I really do not know what advice to give you about invitations to the neighbors, particularly the young females. Are there none of them you could properly [eliminate] without giving offense, and yet to take away the appearance of our thinking ourselves above all our neighbors?"[2] Despite his professed lack of advice, Randolph Harrison plunged ahead into the thicket of wedding etiquette. "As to Jack Page," he continued, "I should not think it right to ask him,

---

1. Harrison's fiancée was born on September 10, 1804.
2. Randolph Harrison to Mary Randolph Harrison, January 21, 1827, Harrison Family Papers, VHS.

to leave out Harry, and being both married men, I see no necessity for asking either."[3] At the same time, however, he was quick to suggest additional names for the wedding invitations and continued with an aside that recurred in much Harrison correspondence: "I am delighted to hear that our dear Poll is recovering her health so rapidly."[4]

Polly had expressed concern about the music at the wedding, and her father had given in, although he noted that, "to indulge Polly in her wish...was to me the greatest difficulty. I think that where so many young people are collected, it is better for them to dance than not, besides the pleasure I take in gratifying our child."[5] As for the guests, "you must take care," he warned, "to avoid giving cause of displeasure by neglecting such of our neighbors as you think ought to be invited... They can go home at night and the rest can tumble about as they can. The number will perhaps be so great that they cannot be lodged. I suppose we must have card tables, and that will amuse them."[6]

No record survives of the marriage that joined the two branches of the Harrison clan. What is known is that on February 8, 1827 the young couple was united in marriage, and the house at Upper Brandon, itself only about two years old, had acquired its first mistress.[7]

In the early nineteenth century the Harrisons and other prominent James River families maintained in considerable style the reputation for hospitality that Virginia plantation society had earned in the colonial period. Their fashionable entertainments drew frequent comments from travelers, like the New Englander who in 1833 remarked on the "princely hospitality of the gentle-born families" of Virginia.[8] Whether socializing consisted of simple house calls, elaborate dinner parties, or the grandest occasion, the wedding party, the families of Upper Bran-

---

3. Ibid.
4. Ibid.
5. Randolph Harrison to Mary Randolph Harrison, January 11, 1827, Harrison Family Papers, VHS.
6. Ibid.
7. *VMHB*, XXXV (1927), 455.
8. Virginius Dabney, *Virginia: The New Dominion* (Garden City, N.Y., 1971), p. 255.

don, Shirley, Westover, Berkeley, Weyanoke, and other plantations maintained frequent and agreeable contact with their neighbors.[9]

Not all Virginians viewed this legendary hospitality with pride. The Harrisons' neighbor, curmudgeon Edmund Ruffin, believed that the "hospitality of old Virginia" was as much the cause of economic decline as agricultural backwardness was. With characteristic exaggeration, Ruffin decried the "custom to give up to all our visitors not only the best entertainment but also the time, the employments and the habits of the host—and this not only to friends and visitors—but for every individual of the despicable race of loungers and spongers which our custom of universal hospitality has created."[10] Because of his high opinion of William Byrd Harrison's management of Upper Brandon, it is unlikely Ruffin had his neighbor in mind when he made this statement. Whatever evidence Ruffin may have had for making his sweeping indictment, he ignored the value of the extensive round of social calls in plantation life. Such entertainments were, in addition to purely social occasions, the means by which information was circulated, the isolation of rural life overcome, marriage alliances among plantation families formed, and a way of life perpetuated.

The evidence we have about dinner parties at the great plantations gives some indication of the importance of these events in the lives of the plantation owners. A participant in one such evening at Weyanoke plantation, just across the river from Upper Brandon, describes the activities. "While at Brandon I went with the family to dine at Douthats across the river. Shortly after noon with the Harrison gentlemen... we crossed the river here a mile and a half wide in a handsome barge with a pair of negro oarsmen. At the opposite landing we were met by the Harrison carriage which had passed over earlier with the ladies of the family. There were thirty or forty guests gathered at the house...with about two negroes to each white... The conversational entertainment was about as usual at Virginia dinners. For three hours or more the ladies talked among themselves, looked after their children, sewed, knitted,

---

9. For a description of these various levels of plantation socializing, see Ransom Badger True, *Plantation on the James: Weyanoke and Her People, 1607-1938* ([Richmond], 1986), pp. 126-32.
10. Quoted in Dabney, *Virginia*, p. 256.

embroidered, and some of the more intimate friends assisted and counselled in getting up the entertainment. The gentlemen generally kept apart, smoking, chewing, drinking whiskey, talking politics, anecdotes, facetious and frequently coarse. At four dinner was announced and we went in jovially without attempt at ceremony. The dinner was rich, varied and in quantity and continued until seven or eight o'clock. It was ten at night before we took our boat to return home. Our row on a crisp starlit night was exhilerating." [11]

Julia Gardiner Tyler, the hostess at neighboring Sherwood Forest Plantation, described her dinner menu. [12]

Soup:	*Dessert:*
Boiled rock fish	*Sweet Pudding & wine sauce*
Baked shad & roe	*Mince Pie*
Pressed salmon	*Sponge cake 6 lb., implanted*
Preserved Lobster	*with a bunch of hyacinths*
A round of Beef	*Two forms of ice cream*
A Boiled Ham	*Two molds of jelly*
Broiled Turkey & Egg sauce	*Two molds of Blanc mange*
Boiled tongue	*A center stand of soft custard*
Chicken salad	*4 dishes of preserves*
Irish potatoes, mashed a la	
maitre d'Hote	
Green Peas, Spinach, Carrots,	*Wines:*
Rice, Celery, Lettuce &	*Sparkling Hock*
radishes, Parsnips	*2 kinds of Madiera*
	Sherry
	Port

These descriptions reinforce the vision of the "good life" enjoyed by plantation society. An account of a similar visit to Weyanoke, however, hints of a more somber aspect of life in antebellum Virginia. The mistress of Weyanoke, Mrs. Douthat, was entertaining. "We were by invitation at Mrs. Douthat's to dinner yesterday. She had invited a large company

---

11. Quoted in True, *Weyanoke*, p. 127
12. Ibid., p. 128.

but few appeared. Three ladies who were expected were taken suddenly ill and had physicians attending them in the morning."[13] One of these ladies was Mrs. William Byrd Harrison.

Indeed, among the many threads that run through the accounts of life at Upper Brandon in the period between the completion of the great plantation house and the opening guns of the Civil War some thirty-six years later, none is more pervasive than concern for the health of friends and family. Few of the surviving letters go far without mentioning health and, in so doing, casting an indirect indictment on the sad state of medicine, both in prevention and in treatment.

In truth, no one, rich or poor, had much hope in that era of escaping life-threatening illnesses that are easily curable today. This, of course, was an era when only the most desperate surgical procedures were attempted, when diagnosis was difficult, and when treatment consisted of part folklore, part quackery, part poison.[14]

The situation is portrayed in one of William Byrd Harrison's earliest surviving letters, one that is also a testament to the fondness and affection that he felt for his older brother and neighbor, George Evelyn Harrison. Writing to one of his sisters (probably Ann Harrison Byrd), William declared:

> *It is with the most inexpressible satisfaction to myself and the greatest gratitude to the Dispenser of all good, that I am able to communicate to you the glad tidings of our beloved George's being pronounced absolutely out of danger...after an alarming illness... His complaint was a violent, remittant bilious fever.... I cannot describe the horrible anxiety I was in.*[15]

---

13. Ibid., p. 129.
14. Agatha Young, *The Men Who Made Surgery* (New York, 1961). The outbreak of cholera in Virginia in 1833 prompted great concern in the Harrison family. George Evelyn Harrison expressed "apprehension of the cholera appearing there [at Brandon]. It's [sic] ravages among the blacks at Norfolk are horrid. We are using some precautions to keep it off, which I trust will be effectual. William B. Harrison to Ann H. Byrd, September 8, 1833, Byrd Family Papers, VHS. George E. Harrison to Ann H. Byrd, undated but apparently ca. 1833, ibid.
15. William B. Harrison to "Dear Sister," September 13, 1823, Byrd Family Papers, VHS.

Harrison's letter does not indicate what treatment his brother received, nor does his description provide enough information to warrant a guess, although George apparently contracted the illness on a trip from Philadelphia.[16]

Polly's health, in particular, continued to be a cause for frequent concern. In a letter on May 21, 1827, one of Polly's sisters said she was "much concerned to hear that my dear Poll is delicate...as I am deeply interested in all that concerns her, more especially her state of health."[17] By the following month, Polly was either no better or had contracted some other ailment. In a letter to her mother, she said, "Mr. Harrison procured some quinine for me which I took rapidly at Powhatan Ct. House that night and on Wednesday...though looking most cadaverously, I was almost well again."[18] The ingestion of the quinine, she noted, was in response to having been "taken with a chill" while on her way from Upper Brandon to Clifton.[19]

It is also possible that Mrs. Harrison's indisposition had another explanation: she was pregnant. Upper Brandon was about to receive

---

16. The Pennsylvania connection is supported in part by the fact that George had attended college there, apparently Dickinson College in Carlisle (brief biographical sketch of George E. Harrison in the S. Bassett French papers, VSL). The sketch states that Harrison "had none of the ambitions of the politicians, although he took a deep interest in the affairs of his county" and served a term in the Virginia House of Delegates. The account states he was a man who "right nobly did full sway for the benefit of all around him."

17. Jane Cary Fitzhugh Harrison Randolph to Susanna Isham Harrison, May 21, 1827, Harrison Family Papers, VHS.

18. Mrs. William B. Harrison to Mrs. Randolph Harrison (her mother), June 19, 1827, Harrison Family Papers, VHS. Readers may wonder at the identity of the "Mr. Harrison" to whom Polly refers. "Mr. Harrison" is undoubtedly her own husband. To have referred to one's own husband by such a formal address was not unusual, but a sign of respect, even when communicating with members of one's own family.

19. Ibid. Quinine was one of the few specific remedies that had any efficiency at that time. What it was effective against, of course, was malaria, a disease that was not then specifically recognized, but one that was indigenous to areas in which mosquitoes bred. If malaria was indeed the cause of the chills Mrs. Harrison was experiencing, then this may very well have contributed to her later record of continuing illness and physical complaint, because malaria tends to be a recurrent disease and quinine primarily a medium of control rather than cure.

its first heir. On February 5, 1828 Mary Randolph Harrison was safely delivered of a son, Benjamin Harrison Harrison. A little over two months later, Polly's sister, Susanna Isham Harrison, on a visit to Upper Brandon described the baby as "the sweetest thing of his age I ever saw, he is a very handsome baby and coos as sweetly as can be."[20] The child was baptized about two months later.[21]

20. Susanna Isham Harrison to Mary Randolph Harrison, April 21, 1828, Harrison Family Papers, VHS.
21. Elizabeth Page Harrison Powell to Ann H. Byrd, June 18 [no year], in which she wrote, "Mr. Meade made a Christian of little Benjie boy last evening, and Polly, and brother Will requested me to stand godmother for him, I was the only person that they made the request of" Byrd Family Papers, VHS; Virginia Department of Conservation and Economic Development, *A Hornbook of Virginia History* (Richmond, 1947), p. 54. Although it is not specified in connection with this baptism, Upper Brandon, as part of Martin's Brandon parish was served by Merchant's Hope Church, one of the state's oldest.

CHAPTER FIVE

The Demands of Farming and Family

William Byrd Harrison had a new family and a new house, but he also had a plantation to run. We can learn about his problems and successes in the frequent letters he wrote to his father-in-law, Randolph Harrison, of Clifton. Perhaps he found in the older man the confidant his own father might have been, had he lived longer.

> *I regretted very much [wrote William] that we could not join our friends in Mathews, as we proposed to do, in consequence of the carriage I bought requiring some attention to render it altogether fit for the road.... The early wheat is now ripening so fast, that our trip to Mathews....is altogether declined for the present. I shall commence cutting it tomorrow.*[1]

The weather, a concern of farmers since the beginning of agriculture, also troubled young William.

> *We have had a great deal of rain lately; so much that we apprehended great danger of the rust in our wheat, and have found the excessive wet was a great impediment to the proper working of the crop of corn. New clouds are still lowering and portend a continuance of the bad weather. If there be much moor [sic], the wheat must invariably have the rust.*[2]

He spoke of preparing to accompany Polly on a visit to Clifton, even though he noted that "she complained of being a little unwell yesterday, but today she seems to be pretty well again."[3] Regardless, he

---

1. William B. Harrison to Randolph Harrison of Clifton, May 30, 1827, Harrison Family Papers, VHS.
2. Ibid.
3. Ibid.

added, he must return to Upper Brandon "by the time the late wheat is fit for the scythe."[4]

Carriages and crops were not the only things occupying William's thoughts, however. He concluded his letter with a note that "I am not altogether pleased with the pair of horses I purchased in Richmond; tho I dare say it would be difficult to obtain better. They appear to be quite gentle and tame, which are strong recommendations."[5]

The next summer Harrison commiserated with his father-in-law after he learned that the crops at Clifton had been "materially damaged" by heat. Things were little better at Upper Brandon, where "we will make very little moor [sic] than half a crop in this neighborhood."[6] There too the problem was heat:

> *Ten days before harvest the wheat exhibited every appearance of being about to fill well and I calculated on a tolerable crop with great certainty and was most woefully disappointed on returning home from Petersburg after an absence of only two days at finding how much the grain had shrivelled.*[7]

Here also is an early indication of the willingness to experiment to improve crops that marked Harrison's life as a farmer. "I cannot help thinking," he wrote his father-in-law, "in contradiction to your opinion, that the yield would have been greater if the wheat had been cut before it began to shrivel."[8] Unfortunately, William's letters give neither yield per acre nor the number of acres planted, so it is impossible to gauge whether the performance of his crops was really as bad as he maintained or whether he was simply being modest.

This is also one of the few letters in which he mentioned Polly without any indication of poor health. "Polly and Ben—continue quite well,"[9]

---

4. Ibid.
5. Ibid.
6. William B. Harrison to Randolph Harrison of Clifton, July 8, 1828, ibid. It is interesting to note that even William could not break the habit of referring to his plantation by its original name. His letters are frequently headed "Brandon," rather than "Upper Brandon." This may also be because the post office and the main wharf were at Brandon.
7. Ibid.
8. Ibid.
9. Ibid.

he wrote, and a visit to friends at the plantations of Longwood, Sabot Hill, and Dover was planned. The only mention of ill health was a report that his brother, George Evelyn Harrison, had been "very delicate for some time past" but was "fast recovering," with more improvement to be expected from a forthcoming visit to the Virginia Springs.[10]

Eighteen twenty-eight was apparently a quiet, happy time for the young Harrison clan. By the fall, the main concern was that infant Benjamin's "long expected teeth have not yet appeared, which makes him much more fretful and his appetite more wayward than usual."[11] So wrote Benjamin's aunt, Susanna Isham Harrison, to her mother. Susanna's diagnosis of Benjamin's health continued:

> *I believe the cause of his resting badly is that Polly has scarcely any milk and as he sleeps with her the greater part of the night and sucks whenever awake he is provoked at getting so little.... Brother Will is indisposed with a cold but not enough so to confine him to the house.*[12]

Reflecting upon life at Upper Brandon, Susanna observed:

> *It has been raining steadily all day and is really a winters day I think. We have spent a quiet time: except Mr. Harrison occasionally there have been but 3 persons here since we came: we have so many resources within ourselves though that so far from regretting the want of society I never was happier from home and indeed the weeks have flown so rapidly that I feel quite melancholy at the thought of going away.*[13]

The propriety of how her journey home was to be made was of no small concern to Susanna:

> *Thursday fortnight I should like to take the steamboat to Richmond.... It will be a trial to go alone to Richmond. I have observed that the boats do not pass here until after 5 in the*

10. Ibid.
11. Susanna Isham Harrison to Mary Randolph Harrison, November 6, 1828, Harrison Family Papers, VHS.
12. Ibid.
13. Ibid.

This portrait was painted in 1833 by an unknown English artist showing William Byrd Harrison's two oldest sons Randolph Harrison (1829-1900), age 3 and Benjamin Harrison Harrison (1828-1862), age 5 in the garden at Upper Brandon. Their aunt, Elizabeth Page Harrison Powell, reports in a May 9, 1835 letter to her sister, Ann Harrison Byrd that, "Ran and Ben are vastly stout, & amuse themselves with their garden, the boys have fine corn & peas coming on. They are very good schollars, & are coming on finely." Both served the Confederacy during the Civil War. Benjamin was killed at the battle of Malvern Hill across the James River from Upper Brandon on July 1, 1862. Randolph lost his right leg at Hatcher's Run on March 30, 1865, but lived to inherit Ampthill, a home in Cumberland County also owned by his father.

evening, in which case they must be travelling nearly all night:
however if brother Randolph or cousin Tom Drew would meet
me there I shall consider the trip less disagreeable.[14]

Alas, Susanna's trip from Upper Brandon was not to be, at least in the
form she anticipated, for reasons of social convention. "I was to have
taken the steamboat this day," she wrote to her mother, but "my plans
for returning had not been made known to brother Wm.... After seeing
your letter he said I must not undertake the trip alone for he thought
there was great impropriety in it."[15]

The delay for the sake of propriety was complicated, however,
because "Brother William" had engaged a man to survey some newly
purchased property, and George Evelyn Harrison was away "on a trip
to the North." Susanna apprised her mother, however, of Ben and Polly:

> *You would be surprised to see how much Ben has fattened and*
> *improved ...since he was weaned. I do not know why it should*
> *be either for Polly's milk is pure and sweet as it ever was;*
> *...before being weaned he depended...on that [but] now he has*
> *what his nurse calls a most excellent stomach and demolishes*
> *a goodly quantity of food.... I never saw a little fellow bear*
> *weaning better...nevertheless he would suck as freely as ever*
> *if permitted.*[16]

A visit from the doctor had been necessary, Susanna noted, to lance
young Ben's gums, and "today we discover a tooth just peeping out."
Polly, for once, was "very well [and] eats most heartily...[although]
Brother Wm suffers a good deal with a pain in one of his legs which
we think must be rheumatic but he will not do anything for it."[17]

Young Ben was joined on September 26, 1829 by a brother, Randolph,
who was born at Clifton, where his mother was visiting her parents.[18]

---

14. Ibid.
15. Susanna Isham Harrison to Mary Randolph Harrison, December 2, 1828, ibid.
16. Ibid.
17. Ibid.
18. Harrison genealogy, in the possession of Mr. William Byrd Harrison III.

Yet another child was on the way by the following fall, but miscarriage deprived the family of the prospect of an immediate addition.[19]

Less than a year later George Evelyn Harrison and his wife, Isabella Ritchie Harrison, experienced a similar loss. "Imagine then my surprise and distress," wrote George to his sister in September 1831, "to find myself yesterday morning, for a very brief period, a *father*. The babe was a female of not quite seven months & survived about as many hours. We hoped at one time to have saved it but nature forbade.... The dear mother is...more composed than I had supposed."[20]

The cycle of life and death, however, continued at Upper Brandon. So too did the growing expertise of William Byrd Harrison as a scientific farmer.

19. George E. Harrison to Ann H. Byrd, November 8, 1830, Byrd Family Papers, VHS.
20. George E. Harrison to Ann H. Byrd, September 30, 1831, ibid.

CHAPTER SIX

Agriculture and Commerce

In addition to maintaining a close personal and working relationship with his brother at Brandon, William Byrd Harrison established close ties with another neighbor. This was Edmund Ruffin, of Evergreen, the neighboring plantation that lay just upstream from Upper Brandon. Ruffin is remembered today primarily for his fiery defense of the Confederacy and for his advocacy of slavery and states' rights. It was Ruffin who in 1861 in Charleston harbor fired the opening gun of the Civil War. And, in 1865, with the Confederacy destroyed and the Union reunited by force, the same Edmund Ruffin put a rifle in his mouth and killed himself rather than live as a subject of the United States of America.[1]

In one sense, however, Ruffin's social and political ideas overshadow and obscure the complexity of a man whose interests ranged widely. Ruffin was, for example, editor of the *Farmers' Register*, which bore as part of its title the words, "A Monthly Publication Devoted to the Improvement of the Practice, and Support of the Interests of Agriculture."[2]

It was in the pages of Ruffin's journal that William Byrd Harrison made known many of his developing theories of agriculture. In one lengthy article on the use of land, for example, he wrote of employing lime extensively to improve the soil, a practice not generally followed in the agriculture of that day.[3] Harrison's article also showed that he clearly understood the necessity for crop rotation, the absence of which led

---

1. For the life and work of Ruffin, see William K. Scarborough, ed., *The Diary of Edmund Ruffin*, (2 vols.; Baton Rouge, 1972, 1976), Betty L. Mitchell, *Edmund Ruffin: A Biography* (Bloomington, 1981), and David F. Allmendinger, Jr., "The Early Career of Edmund Ruffin, 1810-1840," *VMHB*, XCIII (1985), 127-54.
2. *Farmers' Register*, III (1836).
3. Ibid., p. 241.

Looking east at Upper Brandon's rich farm land, 750 acres nestled within the large loop formed by the meandering James River. These lands are certainly among the oldest under continuous cultivation in the country.

in many parts of the South to impoverished soil, particularly when the crop was cotton. The article also reveals that his view of crop rotation was obtained on a trip to England.[4] Harrison wrote:

> *It is considered there [in England] an established rule, founded on long experience and profound observation, that the more rarely any crop occurs in a rotation, the heavier it will be found to be; and the reason is, that the specific food of the plants constituting the crop, will there be found in sufficient quantities in the soil to nourish them to perfection.*[5]

William Byrd Harrison writing to his sister Ann in 1835 reveals that his satisfaction from achievement of a "good crop" is at least as important to him as making a profit (see footnote 11, page 47).

4. Ibid., p. 243. Harrison's reference to a trip across the Atlantic is enigmatic for the researcher, for nowhere in the available correspondence to or from him or other members of the family is there any reference to what was, in those days, a substantial journey. Edith Tunis Sale, in an article "Upper Brandon" from an unidentified 1930s publication, says Harrison "chartered a ship loaded with corn grown on his plantation" and sent it to relieve the famine in Ireland. No dates are given, but the tone of Sale's article and the fact that the great Irish potato famine occurred in the 1840s suggest this was later than 1836, the time at which Harrison makes his enigmatic reference to having crossed the Atlantic.
5. *Farmers' Register*, III (1836), 243.

Kennon Marsh at the tip of the Upper Brandon peninsula is approximately 450 acres of an estuarine marsh whose cypress trees, smartweed, giant bulrush, arrowhead, buttonbush, creeks and sheltered bays form an inviting habitat for resident and wintering waterfowl. It is home to other wildlife including osprey, owls, herons, muskrat, raccoon, deer and fox, and is a spawning area for anadromous and resident fish such as herring, brim, pickerel and largemouth bass.

Two impressions emerge immediately from a reading of Harrison's work in the *Farmers' Register.* The first, based upon a reading of his correspondence, is that Harrison was far more comfortable—even happier—in writing detailed essays on agriculture than he was in composing personal letters. Providing the obligatory chit-chat and family gossip expected in such letters did not come easily for him. Indeed, his letters sound like they were a struggle to create compared to the relaxed, even flow of the letters of his brother.

The second impression derives directly from the essays themselves: Upper Brandon, like other Virginia plantations, was a working *farm*, an economic endeavor that required great labor and superior management in order to succeed. In that realistic sense, Upper Brandon was the very antithesis of the Hollywood image of plantation life in the antebellum South.

An example of how William Byrd Harrison had an eye to a profitable use of his land is found in an aside in his essay on crop improvement. The reference reveals that a "large marsh" substituted for a standing pasture. Ruffin later identified this area as the margin between Kennon Marsh and the higher land that could be tilled.[6] By using this land as pasture, Harrison was thus able to free other land for crops while still providing sustenance for cattle. Without diminishing the acreage for crops, Harrison made the most of the cycle in which cattle depend on fresh fodder, in order to sustain a sufficient number of them to produce enough manure to be used on corn, wheat, and other crops.[7]

In a very real sense the plantations of the Harrison brothers became laboratories in which they not only applied the theories of Edmund Ruffin but also modified and extended them as "others timidly followed their lead."[8] Ruffin's experiments included the application of marl as a neutralizer of acidic soil, as well as experiments with Peruvian guano, gypsum, lime, and bone. It is incongruous, therefore, that the man who today is remembered primarily as a secessionist firebrand was originally hailed as the "Father of Agricultural Chemistry."[9] "The rise of small-scale farming [and] the introduction of grain-growing and market-

---

6. Ibid., p. 243; X (1842), 276.
7. Francis Earle Lutz, *The Prince George-Hopewell Story* (Richmond, 1957), p. 118.
8. Ibid.
9. Ibid., p. 119.

The wharf at Upper Brandon located just north of the manor house had most likely been in service about fifty years at the time of this photo circa 1880. The wharf was a hub of activity and essential to a thriving plantation.

gardening...were some of the reforms set in motion in their own county by Ruffin and the Harrisons."[10]

Such was the commitment of William Byrd Harrison to quality farming that he occasionally let it at least balance matters of profit and finance. "Our own prospect [for the crops] is not good, but nothing approaching a total failure," he wrote his sister in 1835. "We may yet do very well in point of proceeds, which is after all the point of most consequence—to tell the truth however I had rather make a little less money, and make a good crop—."[11]

Harrison's commercial success depended in part on the location of Upper Brandon, for transportation in Virginia relied on rivers whenever possible until well into the twentieth century. The rivers provided the urban connections essential to the large plantations for which agriculture was not just a matter of subsistence farming but a means of participating in a market economy. Areas such as the Northern Neck, the peninsula bounded by the Rappahannock and the Potomac, frequently had as much social and commercial contact with the port of Baltimore at the head of the Chesapeake Bay as with Virginia cities. For Upper Brandon, which lies about fifty-five miles downstream from Richmond and sixty-five miles upstream from Norfolk, the James was a great highway past its door leading both to the state capital and to the wider world beyond Virginia.[12]

The James was used for commerce with Europe as early as John Martin's day, when the principal export from the river plantations was tobacco.[13] In eastern Virginia by the early 1800s, however, tobacco began to give way to grain crops, principally wheat. In part, events beyond the farms as well as the depletion of soils through over-cultivation of tobacco caused this shift. The creation of a manufacturing base in Richmond, for example, where the largest flour milling establishments in the nation operated in the years just before the Civil War, encouraged nearby plantations to shift to wheat.[14] William Byrd Harrison

---

10. Ibid.
11. William B. Harrison to Ann H. Byrd, June 11, 1835, Byrd Family Papers, VHS.
12. Old Dominion Steamship Line, Norfolk, *A Few Facts With 368 Questions and Answers*, (June, 1889).
13. Robert Polk Thompson, *William and Mary Quarterly*, 3d ser. XVIII, (1961), 400.
14. David R. Goldfield, *Urban Growth in the Age of Sectionalism: Virginia, 1847-1861* (Baton Rouge and London, 1977), p. 187.

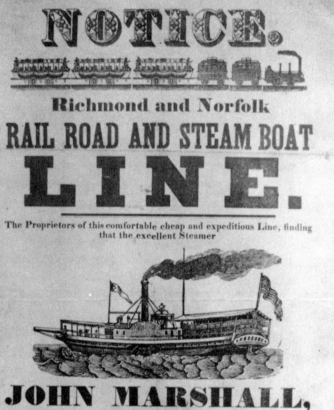

Broadside for the steamboat John Marshall, 1845.

devoted considerable acreage and much attention to his wheat crop, as Edmund Ruffin described in an article on Upper Brandon in the *Farmers' Register.*[15] Although Harrison's other principal crop, corn, could be consumed on the plantation, wheat was a money crop and had to be sold commercially. It is most likely that Upper Brandon wheat found its way by riverboat first to Richmond for milling and then to other cities for sale, shipped by rail or steamboat.

In addition to the development of manufacturing in the capital, the causes of the increase in river traffic past Upper Brandon included the growth in the population of Richmond and other up-river communities and the completion of the James and Kanawha Canal, which was built to promote navigation above the falls. The growth of steamboat companies in the antebellum period eliminated the problems of sailing against wind and current, with the result that by the end of the century more than eight hundred vessels a year entered and cleared at Richmond's customhouse.[16]

As the principal highway for passenger travel as well as commerce, the James brought many visitors within easy reach of the river plantations throughout the nineteenth century and well into the early 1900's. All of the plantations were either regular passenger stops or at least mail stops along the routes of the steamship companies that scheduled service along the James.[17] A typical steamship schedule, published by the Richmond and Petersburg Railroad in 1845, provided for a trip of approximately ten hours from Norfolk to Richmond at a cost per passenger of $2.00.[18]

---

15. *Farmers' Register,* X (1842), pp. 274-82.
16. "The Improvement of James River," a statement issued by a joint committee representing the City Council of Richmond and the Richmond Chamber of Commerce (1898), p. 4 (the library of Virginia House, Richmond). This figure does not include more than two hundred other vessels engaged solely in American traffic that did not require them to clear customs.
17. For an account of the stops made by late nineteenth-century steamboats, see The Virginia Navigation, Co., *Afloat on the James* (Richmond, n.d.).
18. Broadside, February 14, 1845, VHS.

CHAPTER SEVEN

Slavery: An Accepted Cancer in an Honorable Society

The making of a "good crop," which William Byrd Harrison so desired, depended on many things—his own skill and knowledge, his long hours, the agricultural genius of Edmund Ruffin, and the cooperation of the weather. It also depended on tools, equipment, livestock, and most importantly on manpower—and that manpower was provided by the iniquitous institution of slavery.

One of the great paradoxes of American history, as seen from the perspective of the 1980s, is that southern planters, a class that in general set such store in honor, family, freedom and liberty, could tolerate and even defend the institution of human slavery. Slavery in fact had been accepted as a part of civilization for centuries. Similarly, the culture into which the Harrisons of the nineteenth century were born failed to see the contradiction between the principles of Christianity it taught so fervently and the inhumanity of a system of bondage.

The African slave trade had been in existence for sometime when, as noted by John Rolfe in a report to the Virginia Company in London, twenty black slaves were first landed at the Jamestown colony in 1619 by a Dutch ship in exchange for victuals.[1] The first American-built slave ship, the "Desire," sailed from Marblehead, Massachusetts, in 1636.[2] Slavery did not become a widespread, flourishing institution, however, until some years later after the colonists, in much need of manpower, found the labor of Indians and white indentured servants inadequate to their needs. Gradually, they turned to the importation of Africans, who could be bought outright for life and represented a seem-

---

1. Lorome Bennett, Jr., *Before the Mayflower: A History of Black America*, (Chicago, 1967), p. 16.
2. Ibid, p. 18.

ingly inexhaustible supply.[3] The mores of the times offered little in-hibition to the colonists' efforts to secure manpower in this manner. Thus began the American slave trade, which proved to be the most repugnant element of American history, reflecting man's potential for inhumanity to man. Although importation of slaves became illegal when the slave trade on the high seas was ended by law in 1807, the institu-tion of slavery in America remained.[4]

Many heroes of the American Revolution, including George Washington and Thomas Jefferson, were large slaveholders. While Jefferson was known for his favorable treatment of slaves and his antislavery sentiments, Washington appears to have operated his plantations with a slave labor force whose living conditions were less favorable.[5]

When Edmund Ruffin was born in 1794 at Evergreen in Prince George County, his father "owned more than 140 slaves, making him the second largest slaveholder" in the county.[6] The largest slaveholder in the county may very well have been Benjamin Harrison, of Brandon, before the division of his estate between his sons. By 1824 records show Brandon with ninety-three slaves and Upper Brandon with ninety-four, for a combined total of 187.[7]

By the early 1800s some Virginians were beginning to question slavery.[8] Historian William J. Cooper suggests this was being done for two reasons. Abolitionist sentiment in the North had not yet forced the South into a defensive posture, and some Virginians, particularly from the mountainous areas where there were few slaves, were arguing that

---

3. Ibid.
4. Bennett, p. 386.
5. Julius Lester, *To be a Slave*, New York 1968, p. 62: Lorome Bennett, Jr., *Before the Mayflower*, p. 382. It is interesting to note that Massachusetts was the first colony to give statutory recognition to slavery in 1641, followed by Connecticut in 1650 and Virginia in 1661.
6. Mitchell, *Edmund Ruffin*, p. 3.
7. Personal property tax records of Prince George County (microfilm), VSL.
8. It is interesting to note that almost 100 years before the Civil War, certain Virginia colonial leaders such as Benjamin Harrison, Archibald Cary, Edmund Pendleton, R. H. Lee, R. C. Nicholas and Richard Bland, "awake[ned] to the cruelty of the slave trade and to the danger to the Colony and to the damage...[from]...the intro-duction of great numbers of slaves," were petitioning the king, under authority from the House of Burgesses, to check the slave trade. The petition was read to King George III on January 23, 1773 and died (*VMHB*, XVI [1908], 87).

slavery was "injurious to the economy of the state and to the mores of its white citizens."[9]

With but one significant exception, no record of slave life at Upper Brandon has survived. This exception was a published debate between the Harrison brothers and an English visitor who wrote an account that condemned slavery in general and as it existed at the Brandons in particular. The exchange began innocently with the hospitality the owners of the river plantations normally extended to visitors from far and wide.

In this case the visitor was Charles Augustus Murray, second son of George Murray, the fifth earl of Dunmore and Virginia's last royal governor, who came to the United States in 1834.[10] After three years of travel, he returned to England and published an account that provoked a strong reaction from the Harrisons. As he traveled down the James River, Murray wrote,

> *I paid another visit to two gentlemen, brothers...and their hospitality to strangers is not surpassed in any country that I have seen. Here, too, I saw again walls adorned with the powdered heads and laced coats of our common ancestors. I sat at dinner beneath the sweet smile of Pope's Miss Blount, from the pencil of Sir G. Kneller."[11]*

Murray commented scathingly on slavery, slaves, and the quality of the lower classes of white farmers, although he did admit that concerning the Harrisons he was "gratified...to witness the comparative comfort and good usage enjoyed by their slaves."[12] According to Murray,

> *The huts in which [the slaves] reside are...of wood...divided ...by a compartment [with] a chimney to convey the smoke from*

---

9. William J. Cooper, *Liberty and Slavery: Southern Politics to 1860* (New York, 1983), p. 182.

10. Katharine M. Jones, *The Plantation South* (Indianapolis, 1957), p. 31.

11. Ibid., p. 33. This seemingly innocuous reference to a portrait establishes that Murray was visiting Upper Brandon. Writing in the *William and Mary Quarterly* (2d ser., X [1930], 340), W. S. Morton includes a communication to Hugh Blair Grigsby, a Harrison family friend, from William Ritchie, at Brandon, July 11, 1870, that lists Pope's Miss Blount as one of the "old pictures at Upper Brandon."

12. Jones, *Plantation South*, p. 33.

each division; their food (consisting chiefly of fish, broth, maize
cooked after various fashions, bacon & c.) is wholesome and
sufficient; their clothing, coarse, but suited...their labour...not
beyond their power.[13]

Murray placed the slave population on the Harrison plantations at about 250, a total that does not seem at significant variance with existing tax records. He set at six the effective strength of white men on the estates.[14]

Although he personally witnessed no corporal punishment of slaves, the Harrison's British visitor asserted that each overseer was armed with a cowhide lash. There was no doubt about the use of these instruments. One overseer "with whom I held a long conversation... [said] he was obliged constantly to use the lash, both to the men and women: that some he whipped four or five times a week."

Murray quoted the overseer further as saying that he was "extremely sorry that the [Negro] race existed in Virginia, destroying as they must the market for the white man's labour; [and adding] that the...estate would produce more clear revenue if the property was divided into farms under lease," particularly in view of the price of the average male slave being about 150 pounds sterling (or about $750). Murray disagreed with his informant, at least in part, contending that whites suffered more than Negroes from various fevers, "so that the choice must lie between slavery and free-black labour, of which most Virginians speak as an impracticable theory."[15]

With George Evelyn Harrison as the spokesman, the Harrisons issued a rebuttal that appeared in a volume published in 1836 and was subsequently reprinted in Edmund Ruffin's periodical the same year.[16] Some details about the lives of slaves at Brandon can be gleaned from Harrison's account. Harrison, as a creature of his time, attempted to explain away the evils of the institution by arguing that he treated his slaves well.

---

13. Ibid.
14. Ibid., pp. 33-34.
15. Ibid.
16. J. K. Paulding, *Slavery in the United States* (New York, 1836); see also *Farmers'*
    Register, IV (1837), 180-83.

Often using the word "servants" or "people" as synonyms for slaves, Harrison cited numerous instances of loyalty shown to him and to other masters on the part of bondsmen. "I never lock the outer doors of my house," he wrote. "It is done, but done by the servants... I leave home periodically for two months and commit the dwell-house, plate, and other valuables to the servants, without even an enumeration of the articles."[17]

With regard to working conditions, Harrison wrote that *"the people,* as we generally call them, are required to leave their houses at daybreak, and work until dark... with the intermission of half an hour at breakfast, and one to two hours at dinner, according to the season and sort of work." Slaves were prohibited from leaving the estate without permission, "though they often transgress, and with impunity; except in flagrant cases. Those who have wives on other plantations visit them on specified nights." Harrison enumerated the many different kinds of animals and crops he allowed the slaves to raise and indicated that he purchased much of what they produced. Portions of the marsh were parcelled out so that different slaves could trap muskrats there.[18]

With the memory of a recent slave uprising still fresh, however, Harrison noted that "the negroes are indebted [to the rebels] for a curtailment of some of their privileges. As a sincere friend to the blacks, I much regretted the reckless interference of these persons, on account of the restrictions it has become, or been thought necessary, to impose."[19] This statement was obviously delivered with perfect sincerity. Harrison would likely have felt hurt, and perhaps insulted, had any of his contemporaries suggested that his practices toward blacks hardly constituted friendship.

In his attempt to justify the harshness of the slave system, Harrison inadvertently revealed the oppressive regimentation of the slaves' lives that the institution imposed. Among the restrictions placed on slaves, Harrison's account reveals, was one that forbade them "to preach except to their fellow-slaves, the property of the same owner; to have public funerals, unless a white person officiates; or to be taught to read and

---

17. *Farmers' Register,* IV (1837), 181.
18. Ibid.
19. Ibid.

write." As a substitute, Harrison noted that "my brother and I, who own contiguous estates, have lately erected a chapel on the line between them, and have employed an acceptable minister of the Baptist persuasion." Harrison also made plain his feelings on literacy. "Except as a preparatory step to emancipation, I consider it extremely impolitic...to permit them to read and write: 'Where ignorance is bliss,' 'tis folly to be wise."[20]

Harrison also attempted to make a case as to the well-being of his slaves by describing their working conditions and the food and clothing issued to them. Men received a basic allotment of twelve quarts of Indian meal, seven salt herrings, and two pounds of smoked bacon or three pounds of pork each week. The food was usually issued daily and was supplemented with vegetables, lard, and molasses as available. Invalid or retired slaves drew provisions once a week, and a half pound of lard and eight quarts of meal were provided to each child when it was weaned. The standard issue of clothing for field slaves (house slaves being more finely clad) was a winter coat and trousers, three shirts, a "stout pair" of shoes and socks, a pair of summer pantaloons every year, a hat "about every second year" and a greatcoat and blanket every third year.[21]

When ill, slaves were taken to what Harrison described as a "spacious and well-ventilated hospital." There they are received by an attentive nurse [who has] medicine, additional bed-clothing [and] as much light food as she may require. Wine,...rice, and other little comforts...are always kept on hand. The condition of the sick is much better than that of the poor whites, or free colored people, in the neighborhood." As to punishment, Harrison admitted that "vicious and idle servants are punished with stripes, moderately inflicted."[22] By admitting the need for corporal punishment, Harrison revealed that his slaves were by no means content with their lot.

---

20. Ibid.
21. Ibid., p. 182.
22. Ibid.

To the modern ear, Harrison's defense of the treatment and management of slaves at the Brandon plantations appears to be a self-serving rationalization by a man unable to separate personal economic interest from an intolerable system of bondage. His slaves, had they a voice, would have painted a totally different picture. His slaveowning contemporaries, however, operating in a system supported by law, would undoubtedly have labeled his final statement as moderate: "I do not regard negro slavery, however mitigated, as a Utopian system, and have not intended to so delineate it. But it exists, and the difficulty of removing it is felt and acknowledged by all save the fanatics."[23] With that summary, George Evelyn Harrison perhaps reached a public accounting with which he, his contemporaries, and Murray might well have agreed. The only voice left silent was that of the slaves themselves.[24] That silence, enforced by a system that prevented literacy, results in the sad omission from this story of the identities of the black families of Upper Brandon and their contributions to the productivity and economic growth of the plantation.

In August 1831 an incident occurred that shocked Upper Brandon, along with all of Virginia and the rest of the South. In that month in neighboring Southampton County a slave named Nat Turner led a bloody insurrection, killed between fifty and seventy whites, and ultimately brought about his own death and that of most of his followers.[25]

Like his neighbors, William Byrd Harrison reacted to the rebellion with strong emotion:

> *There is so much excitement and alarm in consequence of the insurrection...felt here that I do not like to leave my family... until perfect tranquility is restored. It is believed that this rising was intended to be general and that this was to have been the*

---

23. Ibid.
24. George Evelyn Harrison is credited by the Virginia State Library with authorship of a short piece in *Farmers' Register* (II [1835], 703), which is signed "A Southron," in which he offered other comments about slave life, in this case their housing. This, he says, should "combine thorough ventilation with...warmth. Candor...[states] that in too many of our Negro-quarters it is wholly unnecessary [to admit] fresh air."
25. Ibid., pp. 181-82. Turner and many of his followers lost their lives, either as the rebellion was put down or afterward as convicted murderers.

day instead of last sunday when by a mistake of the 3d for the
4th sunday the miscreants...prematurely commenced their
operations— They murdered as you have seen from the publick
prints about 64 white persons...[and] have been all taken or
destroyed, but a few who are so surrounded in a swamp by a
large body of men that it is considered impossible for them
to escape.[26]

After describing the alarm that spread throughout Virginia's Southside
and the dispatch of forces by the governor, Harrison continued to give
vent to his rage:

Many of the Negroes behaved very nobly. One refused to join
them though they threatened to kill him if he did not. He was
overheard by one of the whites to tell them...that they might kill
him if they pleased, but he would not join them. John Y. Mason's
family was saved by his negroes... The ringleader is an old man
and a baptist preacher, and has not been yet taken, but he
cannot escape.[27]

After describing a false alarm of slave insurrection in Petersburg,
Harrison somewhat incongruously went immediately into a discussion
of the purchase of another slave, who, he said, "will be treated well
as long as he behaves so."[28]

Harrison's analysis clearly showed little understanding of the under-
lying causes of Nat Turner's insurrection nor its ultimate importance
to the future of the United States. Author W. S. Drewry wrote that,
"Nat Turner's insurrection was a landmark in the history of slavery...
It was the forerunner of the great slavery debates, which resulted in
the abolition of slavery in the United States and was, indirectly, most
instrumental in bringing about this result."[29]

---

26. William B. Harrison to Ann H. Byrd, August 28, 1831, Byrd Family Papers, VHS.
27. Ibid.
28. Ibid.
29. Bennett, *Before the Mayflower*, p. 125.

CHAPTER EIGHT

A Fragile Life Cycle

Although the 1830s and 1840s were times of growth and success for Upper Brandon, they were also decades of deeply felt personal tragedy.

Polly's mother, for whom both she and her husband had a warm, genuine, and continuing affection, died in October 1835. George Evelyn Harrison described the feelings of daughter and son-in-law in a letter written from Clifton, where many branches of the family had apparently gathered:

> *This morning put Brother Will & Polly winding their melancholoy [sic] way to Upper Brandon. The latter was in deep mourning for her excellent mother. It is grievous to think how much the poor lady suffered. Her agony was excruciating, occasioned by paralysis of the bowels (I know of no paraphrases by which I can convey the idea.)* [1]

What the disease may have been we have no way of knowing, but it sounds suspiciously like cancer, or perhaps appendicitis.

The next death struck at William and George's own generation. Their sister, Elizabeth Page Harrison Powell, died November 19, 1836 of "pulmonary consumption," a term that by modern-day standards might refer to pneumonia but was more likely to have been tuberculosis. [2] George wrote that

> *All our apprehensions in regard to...sister Lizzie have been realized. The dear creature died this morning at 10 minutes*

---

1. George E. Harrison to Ann H. Byrd, October 21, 1835, Byrd Family Papers, VHS.
2. George E. Harrison, obituary notice of Elizabeth Page Harrison Powell, ibid.

before 7 o'clock. She retained her senses to the last; and so con-
siderate and kind was she, that, only a few minutes before her
blessed spirit took its flight, she requested cousin Abby and sister
Walker to leave the room, lest by their sobbing... they might
disturb my dear Belle, whose situation is very critical and who
occupied the room just beneath her.[3]

He wrote the same day to Dr. Robert Baldwin, of Winchester, asking
that he and his lady "impart the painful intelligence to my sister Anne
in the way which you may deem least likely to inflict an unnecessary
shock." "I believe," wrote Harrison, that Lizzie was "as well prepared
for the awful transition as any being that ever lived."[4]

Two months later, fire struck the Winchester home of Ann and her
husband, Richard Byrd. There were no deaths, however, and William
tried to console his sister by pointing out, "what for instance would the
loss of a house be regarded by either you or me in comparison with
the death of one of your precious boys?"[5]

Both Harrison brothers were productive, however, during this time
of stress and loss, as were their wives. On October 1, 1837, Polly gave
birth to a namesake for his father, another William Byrd Harrison.[6]
Just a few months earlier Isabella Ritchie Harrison, George's wife, had
given birth to a first child, George Evelyn, Jr., of whom his proud father
wrote, "He delayed making his appearance so long that we began to
fear there was some mistake in the business."[7]

The affection between the families of William and George Harrison
was not just a result of the proximity of Upper Brandon to Brandon.

---

3. George E. Harrison to Richard Evelyn Byrd, November 19, 1836, ibid. There is no
   indication nature of the illness of Isabella, Harrison's wife, although she was to
   make a full recovery.
4. George E. Harrison to Dr. Robert Baldwin, November 19, 1836, ibid.
5. William B. Harrison to Ann H. Byrd, June 21, 1837, ibid. In a letter a few months
   earlier, George had expressed concern that his nephews had not had the measles
   and neither had Polly. "They have," he added at that time, "had the luck of being
   exposed to eruptive disorders. You remember their fight about the smallpox."
   George E. Harrison to Ann H. Byrd, July 22, 1835, ibid.
6. Harrison genealogy in the possession of William Byrd Harrison III.
7. George E. Harrison to Ann H. Byrd, June 22, 1837, Byrd Family Papers, VHS.

It was warm, deep, and genuine family love, and it is illustrated in a letter William wrote from Richmond to his sister Ann. In writing of how he missed Polly and his own family, he recalled how "nephew George Evelyn, the younger, continues to thrive marvelously" and how he had delivered a present into "young Geo. E.'s dear little paws."[8]

During much of this time there was also good reason for the family to be alarmed about the health of William Byrd Harrison. He received news of the decline in Lizzie's health, in fact, while he was himself undergoing treatment at the Blue Sulphur Spa, one of the Virginia mountain resorts to which the privileged and wealthy retired.

His letter expressed concern that Lizzie's lungs might have been affected and offered this graphic portrait of the treatment he received for his own lung disorder:

> *Dr. May prescribed a tartar emetic plaister which afforded me speedy relief. He sprinkled the tartar…upon a Burgundy pitch plaister and directed that it should remain on as long as it could be borne—The pain was very considerable, and on removing the plaister when it became intolerable, I found a good many deep sores under; but the cure had been effected.*[9]

This combination of symptoms and treatments, when considered with Lizzie's symptoms, suggests that tuberculosis may have infected some members of the Harrison clan.

Grievous as the tragedies of recent years had been, however, none could have been harder for William Byrd Harrison to bear than the one that befell him in 1839, two years following the birth of his own namesake and that of his brother. In January of that year George Evelyn Harrison, master of Brandon, died. He was forty-one years old.

The only description that remains is a letter from Thomas Ritchie, George's father-in-law. "We have just consigned George E. Harrison

---

8. William B. Harrison to Ann H. Byrd, November 4, 1837, ibid.
9. William B. Harrison to Ann H. Byrd, September 4, 1836, ibid.

to the tomb of his ancestors," he wrote.[10] Again, the cause of death can only be surmised.

> *Mr. Harrison was seized with the congestive...and no medicine which they administered could arrest it. I do not think he was conscious for 5 days because he sank rapidly until the close of the scene.... Wm. Harrison, the noble Representative of his Brother's virtues, has proved & will prove the best friend of is bereaved wife. She is determined to carry out her Husband's wishes.*[11]

And yet the cycle of death was not over. In 1842, Ann Harrison Byrd, beloved sister and frequent correspondent of both George and William, died. Within six years, William Byrd Harrison had lost his brother and both of his sisters.

---

10. Thomas Ritchie to Richard Evelyn Byrd, January 21, 1839 [misdated 1838], Byrd Family Papers, VHS.
11. Ibid. Edmund Ruffin gives the date of Harrison's death as 1839 (*Farmers' Register*, X [1842], 275), while Ritchie's letter describing his death is clearly and unmistakably dated 1838. Because it is unlikely that the tombstone and Ruffin would both be in error, it seems probable that the mistake must lie with Ritchie, even though he had just attended the funeral. Most likely, he made the same mistake people still make today—writing last year's date on much of their correspondence throughout the first month of the new year, particularly when under stress. January 1839 should therefore be accepted as the correct date.

CHAPTER NINE

Expanding Responsibilities

After the crushing loss of his brother, William Byrd Harrison assumed responsibility for much of the management of Brandon while continuing with his own affairs at Upper Brandon.

The two plantations continued to attract attention as models of modern agricultural management. In 1842, Edmund Ruffin made a detailed report on the plantations to the State Board of Agriculture, in which he noted that the death of George Evelyn Harrison "did not, as is usual in such cases, put a stop to the then well advanced progress of improvement on his estate. His property was placed, and has since continued, under the general supervision and controlling advice of his younger brother."[1] According to Ruffin, Harrison cultivated Upper Brandon as two separate farms. One, known as Upper Brandon, included 780 acres of arable land plus the 1,000 acres of Kennon Marsh. The other, known as Upper Quarter, included 650 acres of arable land and 130 acres of pasture, plus an adjacent 400 acres of woodland.[2] The cycles of crop rotation that Harrison employed differed between the two farms. Upper Brandon farm used a four-field rotation of corn, wheat, clover, and wheat again, while the Upper Quarter farm followed a three-field rotation of corn, wheat, and clover.[3]

Ruffin cited with pride production figures for Upper Brandon that would embarrass a modern farmer with access to chemical fertilizers, irrigation, and pesticides. The best crop of wheat (1838) was twenty-four bushels to the acre, with an average of about fifteen bushels on the Upper Brandon farm and sixteen bushels to the acre at the Upper Quarter farm. The best corn crops averaged seven barrels (thirty-five

---

1. *Farmers' Register*, X (1842), 275.
2. Ibid., p. 276.
3. Ibid.

bushels) to the acre at Upper Brandon farm in the best year (1840), and eight barrels at the Upper Quarter farm.[4]

Ruffin's highly detailed account gives a thorough picture of a working plantation. Livestock included approximately seventy-five cattle at each of the four farms with "the cattle on the lower estate...of...[the] better quality."[5] Harrison did not raise cattle for income, however, except for the sale of about 100 pounds of butter from Upper Brandon and 150 from Brandon. They served primarily as sources of food for human consumption and manure for fertilizer. Approximately 120 sheep, exclusive of lambs, were raised at Upper Brandon at the time of Ruffin's visit, 140 at Brandon. "Very unsuccessful," was Ruffin's comment with regard to hogs at Upper Brandon, where no more than seventy were available for slaughter each year.[6]

Also during this period Harrison apparently took control of yet another plantation, Ampthill, a property near Cartersville in Cumberland County belonging to his father-in-law and not far from his in-laws' home. He immediately began concentrating on agriculture at Ampthill, including the planting of tobacco.[7]

The period of the early 1840s, when the success of his farming operations was blotted by the death of so many loved ones, must have been a time of great stress for Harrison and may have helped account for the silence that fell upon him. The death of so many relatives in the space of a few years, and the burdens of responsibility he felt both for his wife's family and his brother's, left him little time or inclination to correspond with anyone. As he noted in a letter to his beloved sister, Ann, shortly before her death, "I have so many things to occupy my time, and my distaste for writing is so great."[8]

---

4. Ibid., p. 279. Current yields at Upper Brandon average 60 bushels per acre for wheat, 120 bushels per acre for corn, and 50 bushels per acre for soybeans.
5. Ibid., p. 280.
6. Ibid., p. 281.
7. William B. Harrison to Ann H. Byrd, August 6, 1840, Byrd Family Papers, VHS. See also the deed of land sale at Cumberland County Courthouse.
8. William B. Harrison to Ann H. Byrd, April 30, 1841, Byrd Family Papers, VHS.

Ann's final illness was a severe blow. Writing from Ampthill, Harrison said, "I am truly grieved to hear that there is no material improvement in your health. I love you so dearly."[9] There were three other events, however, that once more stressed the cycle of birth and death. Another son, Charles Shirley Harrison, was born March 3, 1842 at Upper Brandon, and a fifth son, George Evelyn Harrison, named for the late master of Brandon, was born August 30, 1844 at Ampthill. On July 16, 1846, however, just a few weeks short of his ninth birthday, the son he had named after himself, William Byrd Harrison, died. For the elder William Byrd Harrison, death had moved past his generation and that of his parents and was striking at his children. He was now forty-six years old. Upper Brandon and the other plantations for which he was responsible were thriving on his hard work and foresight.[10] Events he could not control, however, were closing in on his way of life, his state, and his nation. Although the immediate future still held flashes of joy and moments of great happiness for him, the long shadows were beginning to fall across both his land and his people.

---

9. William B. Harrison to Ann H. Byrd, July 28, 1841, ibid.
10. Two surviving documents testify to Harrison's love of the land. The documents are "On the Cultivation of Corn" and "Comparative Effects of Lime and Marl-Burnt Clay" and both appear in the *Farmers' Register* (I [1834], 395-96), under Harrison's name. The former discusses how to gain maximum yield for minimum labor by planting an even crop that need not be plowed extensively. The other article discusses the application of seventy bushels of unslaked lime per acre on one parcel, 140 bushels of marl on another. Clover appeared to have benefited more from the marl. Ruffin, in another article in the *Farmers' Register* (X, [1842], 276) describes the Brandon lands as generally of a "reddish-brown loam, well known by the provincial term 'mulatto land.'" The lack of natural lime in these soils, he contends, allowed the growth of two unwanted grasses, sheep sorrel (*rumex acetocella*) and poverty grass (*aristida gracilis*).

CHAPTER TEN

A Loving Marriage Passes: Upper Brandon Acquires a New Mistress

Despite his many Virginia responsibilities, in the 1850s William Byrd Harrison was still given to travel and to involvement in a variety of affairs. In August of 1850 he traveled to Baltimore in connection with some type of litigation. Although able to accompany her husband, Polly was "quite an invalid."[1] Other legal problems needed attention in Richmond, as well as back in Prince George County, where concerns about the administration of the estate of his sister Lizzie lasted for many years after her death.

His correspondence with Richard Evelyn Byrd, the widower of his beloved sister, was not always serious, however. Early in 1851, for example, he wrote:

> Do contradict, if you can, a rumour that is going the rounds of the neighbourhood which I consider very prejudiced to your character as a gentlemen of the old school. It is currently reported and by many...believed to be unquestionable,—that R. E. Byrd & a Lady of the City of Winchester were seen on board a steamboat, called the Augusta, at the Brandon wharf between the hours of 11 and 12 o'clock yesterday, and that the said Byrd did, willfully, unreasonably and against all the laws of propriety recognized in the neighbourhood continue on board said steam boat, as if afraid by landing he might put him self within the jurisdiction of Wm. B. Harrison.[2]

---

1. William B. Harrison to Richard Evelyn Byrd, August 10, 1850, Byrd Family Papers, VHS.
2. William B. Harrison to Richard Evelyn Byrd, April 4, 1851, ibid.

Byrd had apparently acquired a new wife, and thus was the butt of Harrison's jest for not having stopped for a visit. That the letter was written in good humor is made clear by Harrison's closing comment: "Polly joins me in warmest regards to Mrs. B—and yourself.... Yours very affectionately."[3]

The years 1850-51 also saw a change in the population of Upper Brandon when the number of adult slaves dropped from ninety-five to eighty-three.[4] Whether this was the result of Harrison selling off some of the slaves or of death from some type of epidemic cannot readily be determined. From an examination of tax records, however, it appears likely that a sale was the cause of the decline because the number of adult slaves at Upper Brandon was maintained at eighty-three in the years 1853, 1855, and 1858. It would have hardly been in keeping with Harrison's careful plantation management to keep more slaves than were necessary.

By 1856, there were deep concerns about Polly, whose entire life had been marked with complaints of ill health. This time, a genuine decline had set in. A letter from Baltimore, where business again had apparently taken Harrison, said he was "almost in despair" over Polly's condition.[5]

The following March two members of the family expressed their concern in a letter to a third. George, now thirteen, wrote his twenty-seven-year-old brother, Randolph, that their mother "had a worse night than usual."[6] In a postscript to young George's letter, written the following day, Mary Randolph Page Harrison, Benjamin's wife, wrote that "Papa

---

3. Ibid.
4. Personal property tax records of Prince George County (microfilm), VSL.
5. William B. Harrison to Abby Byrd Nelson, September 24, 1856, McGuire Family Papers, VHS. Polly's lengthy illness did not keep the Harrison clan tied to her side, however. One of her older sons—probably Randolph, because Ben's presence is alluded to in the correspondence of his wife—was in Europe for a time. A letter from another son, Charles Shirley Harrison inquired, "How are the Turks and Russians coming on?" an apparent allusion to the Crimean War and an implication that Randolph may have been in proximity thereto (Charles Shirley Harrison to his brother, March 11, 1854, original in the possession of William Byrd Harrison III).
6. George Harrison to Randolph Harrison, March 3, 1857, Harrison Family Papers, VHS.

thinks that [Polly's] increased indisposition was caused by a very sudden change in the weather."[7]

Less than six months later, after thirty years of marriage, William Byrd Harrison's beloved Polly died. "My hour of darkness has come," Harrison wrote that day, "but there is a light above me and I feel perfect [assurance] that my darling—she that I loved better than anything mortal—has gone straight to heaven—and I feel a strong hope too that grace will be given me so to lead the residue of my life that I may have a happy reunion with her in heaven." He continued "I did not think that this blow would have been so crushing—prepared as I was by the intense and long protracted sufferings of my darling.... I would not have her back if I could, to languish for a few weeks longer on a bed of suffering...it is, better as it is and yet the [separation] is terrible to bear—."[8] The words of his letter, written on the day of Polly's death, convey a sense of purest pain and deepest loss. Harrison was now fifty-seven years old and had surely experienced his share of suffering in the death of loved ones.

And yet, Harrison did not let his bereavement keep him isolated. Less than a year later, in September 1858, Edmund Ruffin wrote in his diary, "reached the White Sulphur Springs at 12...[and]...looked about to find what friends we had here. There are...Wm. B. Harrison of Prince George (who is avowedly seeking for a second wife)."[9] Two months later Ruffin also wrote of encountering Harrison on a James River ship bound upstream from Norfolk.[10] The following year Harrison, then serving as a member of the Board of Visitors of the College of William and Mary, was named to a special committee to consider construction matters at the college, further evidence that he was making room in his life for responsibilities and, perhaps, pleasures that lay beyond his estates.[11]

---

7. Ibid. Postscript written by Mary Randolph Page Harrison to Randolph Harrison.
8. William B. Harrison to Abby Byrd Nelson, September 22, 1857, McGuire Family Papers, VHS.
9. Scarborough, ed., *Ruffin*, I, 228.
10. Ibid. p. 247.
11. Faculty minutes, College of William and Mary, Mar. 1859, in *William and Mary Quarterly*, 2d ser., VIII (1928), 270.

Included among the latter was a proposal of marriage accepted by Ellen Wayles Randolph, a great granddaughter of Thomas Jefferson. Mary Randolph Page Harrison, William's daughter-in-law and wife of his firstborn, wrote of preparations for the arrival of Upper Brandon's new mistress:

> *Papa is to be married on the 10th of May [1859], and as you may suppose, I am and shall be as busy as a bee, getting things in nice order for Ellen's reception. Of course, I am anxious to have everything in the house, yard & garden in tip-top order—when I deliver up the keys, as I shall do so soon as she comes. Papa wants me to keep them and* entertain *her for a while in* her own house, *but I beg to be excused.*[12]

Although Mary and her husband, had remained at Upper Brandon after Polly's death out of a sense of loyalty, they were anxious to return to their own home:

> *We (Ben and I and our little ones) will remain here a short time after her arrival, then go over bag and baggage to our own little house on the other side of the River. Oh! You don't know how happy I shall be at being in my own house! I had rather live in a log cabin that was* mine, *than in a palace that belonged to* anyone else! *Dear Papa has been like an own father to me...and I would not for a great deal have him know it, but my living here has been great trial to me! ... I have not talked of it even to Ben, because I believed we were doing our duty.*[13]

The wedding was held at Edgehill, Ellen's family home in Albemarle County near Charlottesville and Thomas Jefferson's Monticello.[14]

---

12. M. R. Harrison to unspecified aunt, April 11, 1859, Dame Family Papers, VHS.
13. Ibid.
14. *Petersburg Daily Express*, May 16, 1859.

Even marriage did not keep William Byrd Harrison at Upper Brandon, however. In late July, Edmund Ruffin recorded a conversation with Harrison, Governor J. L. Manning of South Carolina, and others in Richmond concerning debate on "reopening of the African slave trade."[15] Less than a month later, Ruffin was back at White Sulphur Springs where he noted that among the 1,200 visitors were Harrison "and lady."[16]

As the decade of the 1850s drew to a close, on the horizon were events that would make a national name for Ruffin while effectively destroying the economy and system of life at Upper Brandon and hundreds of other plantations like it across the South.

The first event was secession. The second was war.

---

15. Scarborough, ed., *Ruffin*, p. 325.
16. Ibid., p. 330.

CHAPTER ELEVEN

The Civil War:
Sacrifice of Family to a Lost Cause

The increase in sectional tension and the growing threat of civil war distressed many southerners, like Harrison, who had friends and associates in the North. Although many years had passed since his days at Harvard, Harrison had maintained his contacts. Among his correspondence from the secretary of the Class of '20, for example, is a letter expressing sympathy to Harrison on the loss of Polly.[1] The fortieth meeting of the class took place in Boston on July 18, 1860.[2] Although Harrison did not attend, he apparently acknowledged receipt of the announcement and later received a nostalgic account of the reunion from Joseph Palmer, the class secretary.

> *Although forty years had elapsed since we parted, yet every one remembered you and spoke of you with the most kindly feelings, and pleasant recollections of your good scholarship and gentlemanly deportment during the whole of your college courses. [Alfred W.] Haven [of Portsmouth, N.H.], who sat next to you in recitation room, spoke of the great obligations he [had] to you because you always prompted him when he faltered in his lesson.*[3]

By the spring of 1861, Virginia with some reluctance, followed the Deep South out of the Union. The young Harrison men—Benjamin, Randolph, Charles Shirley, and George—were involved with their cause

---

1. Joseph Palmer to William B. Harrison, October 10, 1858, original in the possession of William Byrd Harrison III.
2. Joseph Palmer, class secretary, invitation to the reunion of the class of 1820, July 3, 1860, ibid.
3. Joseph Palmer to William B. Harrison, July 28, 1860, ibid.

and country. Most became officers, as might have been expected of men of their class, but George Evelyn Harrison, Jr., the only son of his late father, apparently served in a Prince George cavalry unit as a corporal.[4] The organization of the cavalry unit had the support of William Byrd Harrison, who, now sixty-one years old and with no previous military experience, was beyond the age for active service with the regular forces.[5]

In the opening year of the war, the two plantations in Prince George County for which Harrison was responsible were thriving. Brandon had 150 slaves, 130 of whom were over sixteen years old, while Upper Brandon had 105, of whom 95 were over sixteen. Upper Brandon also reported 44 horses, mares, colts, and mules; 71 cattle; 79 sheep; and 165 hogs. Aggregate value of property was placed at $14,255, on which the tax was $228.62. It is interesting to note that for some unknown reason the number of adult slaves at Brandon had almost doubled two years later to 240, while the total at Upper Brandon had increased, but only to 96. A system of valuing slaves had also been instituted, with the result that slaves in 1863 at Brandon were valued at $193,000 and those at Upper Brandon at $62,400.[6]

By the summer of 1862, as the war drew close to Upper Brandon, Harrison and his wife were at Ampthill, in Cumberland, west of Richmond and south of the James. From there he wrote to his cousin Abby on June 30 to announce the birth of a daughter. The child, he wrote, was named Jane Nicholas, "an honest hearted girl that will know and love her father."[7]

In the same letter Harrison noted that he had just read of a brilliant Confederate victory over the Union army and expressed the hope that

4. Richard E. Eppes, a Prince George County physician, to his wife, May 25, 1861, Eppes Family Papers, VHS.
5. George E. Harrison to Randolph Harrison, April 27, 1861, original in the possession of William B. Harrison III.
6. Prince George County Tax Records, 1861 and 1863 (microfilm), VSL.
7. William B. Harrison to Cousin Abby, June 30, 1862, McGuire Family Papers, VHS. A Harrison genealogy gives her birthdate as June 26, 1862 and notes that she was the second child born to Harrison and his second wife; the first a son, Evelyn Byrd, was born March 14, 1860 at Upper Brandon, where he died two days later.

God would grant an early peace. "We are of course in a state of great anxiety about the dear boys....If do not hear from them tomorrow, I will go directly over. What a horrid thing war is.... The Lord in mercy spare my children."[8]

Benjamin Harrison Harrison (1828-1862).

Harrison's prayer was in vain. One day later, his firstborn, Benjamin, was killed in action at the battle of Malvern Hill, in Henrico County, not far across the James from Upper Brandon. He had completed a year's study in mathematics with high honors at the University of Virginia, had been elected a captain in the Charles City Cavalry, and had died from seven wounds received while rallying an infantry battalion

8. Ibid.

and leading a charge, sword in hand. He had been with the infantry instead of his unit because the cavalry was not engaged, and he had left his men under the command of a subordinate in order to assist another officer.[9]

It was thus a costly war for William Byrd Harrison. Among his other sons, George, the youngest, enlisted when he was seventeen in the Richmond Howitzers. Randolph lost his right leg at Hatcher's Run on March 30, 1865 in the closing days of the war while serving as a lieutenant colonel of the 34th Virginia Infantry (Wise's Brigade). Had Randolph heeded the advice of a physician to resign his commission and go home in 1862, he might have avoided his loss. "Staying where you are is doing no good to yourself or country. I think I can give you such a letter as would serve your purposes," the doctor wrote.[10] Charles Shirley Harrison, an artillery captain, was captured at Sayler's Creek in the last major battle in Virginia.[11] In mid-June, he was still being held prisoner even though the war had ended.[12]

Because Union forces controlled most of Tidewater Virginia from very early in the war, the Harrisons moved many of their belongings to Petersburg for storage.[13] This decision may have saved some fur-

---

9. John Lipscomb Johnson, ed., *The University Memorial: Biographical Sketches of Alumni of the University of Virginia Who Fell in the Confederate War* (5 vols. in 1; Baltimore, 1871), pp. 186-88.

10. John Peachy to Randolph Harrison, January 12, 1862, original in the possession of William Byrd Harrison III.

11. Biographical sketch, p. 186, S. Bassett French Papers, VSL; Harrison genealogy, p. 61, in the possession of William Byrd Harrison III. William Glover Stanard, "Harrison of James River," *VMHB*, XXXVII (1929), 81, is the source for the statement about George Evelyn Harrison's military career.

12. Isabella R. Harrison to George Evelyn Harrison, Jr., June 12, 1865, in Stanard, "Harrison of James River," p. 396. This George Evelyn Harrison should not be confused with the George Evelyn Harrison in note 11, above; the former was, of course, the son of the late George Evelyn Harrison, of Brandon, and the latter a son of William Byrd Harrison.

13. Wyatt, *Plantation Houses*, p. 30. This was not the first time old Brandon plantation had seen and felt the invader's presence. In May 1781, during the Revolutionary War, British Major General William Phillips had landed there in a strong gale. He was en route to Petersburg to meet Lord Cornwallis, advancing from the south. Phillips, already ill with fever, died in Petersburg.

nishings; it could not save the homes or much other property.[14] Randolph Harrison, however, spoke with admiration of how his father faced adversity. "He bears his losses with much equanimity, and is the most helpful man I have seen deriving comfort from everything. I wish I was as cheerful as he."[15]

Writing from Ampthill two months before Randolph had praised his father's "serenity," the elder Harrison expressed his sadness at the desecration of his late brother's estate for which he still felt a deep responsibility. "It is dismal to ride about Lower Brandon & witness the desolation." At the same time, however, he noted his pleasure with his newest child, Jefferson Randolph, who was born December 9, 1863 at Ampthill.[16]

---

14. Daily Richmond Enquirer, January 28, 1864, "Rumors—The Enemy On James River— It was reported on yesterday, says the Petersburg "Register" of Tuesday, that Yankees from a gunboat or boats landed on Monday at Lower Brandon, James River, and committed for the first time, on that estate some depredations. The report which was first heard, stated that a large barn on the plantation was burned, but fortunately none of the lately gathered corn crop was in it and that there the mischief stopped. Subsequently, it was reported that all the houses on the estate save one were burned, that the enemy carried off two of the overseers and all of the negroes together with two of the Signal Corps. At what important point of duty the latter were caught, and whether they were taken flagrante delicie, in the act of waving their colors or revolving their lights report did not say. To have it in doubt even that old Brandon has been harried by the Yankees, and its old mansion, rich in a thousand memories of the olden times been destroyed by the Beast, is painful in the extreme and we yet hope that rumor, with her lying tongue exaggerated the mischief done to that place. That some mischief has been lately done not only there, but at other points in that section we do not doubt. And we much fear that this is but the beginning of much mischief on the South side of the lower James before Spring time comes."
15. Randolph Harrison to Harriett Heileman Harrison, May 23, 1864, original in the possession of William Byrd Harrison III.
16. William B. Harrison to "Dear Cousin," March 27, 1864, McGuire Family Papers, VHS.

CHAPTER TWELVE

William Byrd Harrison: Eminent Agriculturist and Devoted Family Man

Several documents have survived that describe the wartime fate of Brandon and Upper Brandon. The mistress of Brandon, the widowed Isabella R. Harrison, described damage to the former a few weeks after the end of the war. "The house was devoid of windows and doors.... These [remaining] are pierced through with numerous Bullet holes. They were evidently used as a target from the Lawn. Half the wainscotting...has been torn down, and most of the oak weatherboarding." A Pennsylvania soldier, sent with Mrs. Harrison as an escort and driver, "could scarce restrain his indignation at the evidences of his Confreres' Barbarism" and he helped "clean up some of the rubbish."[1]

The letter described the loss of every chair and noted that some of the former slaves had remained, but only two cows, four oxen, and a sheep. Mrs. Harrison was convinced the former slaves had sold the remainder of the livestock. "You will be surprised," she continued, "that not one of the house servants wish to return to Brandon."[2] Their departure contrasts sharply with the testimonials of loyalty that the late George Evelyn Harrison had written concerning his slaves some years earlier. Mrs. Harrison's letter concluded with the note that "Uncle Will & Georgie" (William Byrd Harrison and his son, George) were at Upper Brandon.[3]

---

1. Isabella R. Harrison to George Evelyn Harrison, Jr., June 12, 1865, in Stanard, "Harrison of James River," p. 394.
2. Ibid., pp. 394-95.
3. Ibid., p. 396.

William Byrd Harrison did not attempt to restore the mansion at Upper Brandon after the war. Hugh Blair Grigsby, historian and fourth president of the Virginia Historical Society, noted in his diary in July 1870 that he had seen both George and Charles Shirley Harrison on a visit to Upper Brandon and had found the house "very much damaged by the Yankees, every door and window gone, chimney pulled down."[4] The descriptions of Grigsby and others indicate Upper Brandon was not fit for permanent residence, although the fields about the mansion were, as ever, kept in careful cultivation. A visitor writing twenty years after the close of the war spoke of Upper Brandon having been "cruelly damaged...and has never been restored to its former condition." A brief description of Upper Brandon and its grounds also spoke of damage not fully repaired sixty-five years after the war's end. "The garden itself...has never been completely restored, though many old shrubs were left to define certain spots—japonica, althea, lilac and syringa." This same account also referred to "sabre cuts in the old balustrade and the liberal sprinkling of bullet holes in the paneled walls."[5] The alleged saber cuts on the hall stairway banister are still quite evident today.

Two events in the early postwar years showed that although the South was defeated, the admiration of the Harrison family for the men who had led the Confederacy remained strong. The first of these events took place in 1867, when the former Confederate president, Jefferson Davis, stopped at the Brandon wharf on the way from prison at Fort Monroe to a federal court hearing in Richmond. Several of the Harrisons went aboard the steamship "to manifest their devotion."[6]

The second event was a visit in the spring of 1870 by the Confederacy's one untarnishable hero, General Robert E. Lee, who was making his way home from a southern tour during which he had been frequently mobbed and constantly idolized by his former soldiers and their families.

4. Hugh Blair Grigsby, diary, July 21, 1870, Hugh Blair Grigsby Papers, VHS.
5. Francis Otway Byrd, "Upper Brandon," in the James River Garden Club, comp., and Edith Tunis Sale, ed. *Historic Gardens of Virginia* (Richmond, 1930), pp. 39-40.
6. Mrs. Burton Harrison, *Recollections Grave and Gay* (New York, 1912), p. 264.

Writing from Brandon, Lee spoke of having ridden to the "other Brandons" and having seen all the inhabitants. "Mr. William Harrison," he noted in another letter, "[is] much better than I expected to find him." Of himself, he says simply, "I am better, I trust." He was wrong. Before the year was out, both men would be dead.[7]

In the summer of 1870 William Byrd Harrison apparently was back at Ampthill. That plantation had been sanctuary for Harrison during much of the war. It was close to the homes of both his beloved wives. It was where some of his children had been born. And it was there, on September 22, 1870, in his seventy-first year, that he died, apparently from a fall.[8]

The inventory of Upper Brandon seems to show that the estate remained a successful working farm. This is particularly surprising when one considers that the devastations of the Civil War had ended only a few years earlier and that the South had since been subjected to military occupation and Reconstruction.

When one remembers that the personal property tax records of the county in 1860, the year before the war, listed 179 cattle, sheep, and hogs at Upper Brandon, then the comparable figure from 1871 of 291 such animals is remarkable. The inventory also reported a wide assortment of wagons, carts, harrows, reapers, and farm implements. There were also a carriage and horses; the former dating to 1855 and the horses to 1850. The account included a sizable library for those days of some 720 volumes and 493 ounces of silver plate perhaps saved during the family migration to Petersburg. It also noted "Relics from the War (at a most liberal value in worth no more than five hundred dollars)."[9]

---

7. Robert E. Lee, Jr., *Recollections and Letters of General Robert E. Lee* (New York, 1924), pp. 401-03.
8. Statement of George Byrd Harrison (who in 1870 changed his name from George Evelyn Harrison) and C. Shirley Harrison (who was then adopting the modern fad of dropping his first name [Charles] in exchange for an initial), as attached to the inventory of their father's Upper Brandon assets (October 20, 1871), Prince George County Courthouse, Inventory and Accounts Book, pp. 557-58.
9. Ibid.

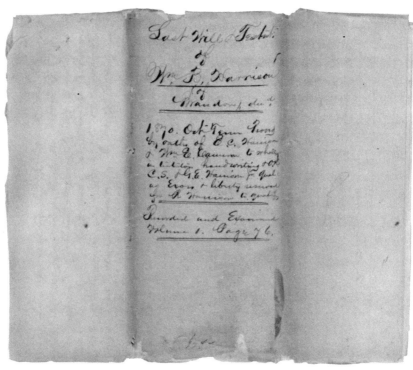

The cover page of William Byrd Harrison's thirteen page will written in his own hand not quite a year before his death, September 22, 1870.

Harrison left a lengthy and complex will, dated 1869, the year before his death.[10] To his wife, Ellen Wayles Harrison, he left the use of his house and property for the balance of her life and a third of the profits from the farms at Upper Brandon. Those farms were divided, primarily between Shirley and George Harrison, although provisions were also made for the children of Harrison's second marriage.

Harrison's omission from the will of Randolph, his other surviving son from his first marriage, is explained by records at the Cumberland County Courthouse. These documents show not only the details of how William Byrd Harrison came into possession of Ampthill, but also that

10. Will of William Byrd Harrison, dated October 26, 1869, Prince George County Courthouse.

this substantial plantation was passed on to Randolph during his father's lifetime and remained in the Harrison family until 1924.[11]

The death of William Byrd Harrison brought statements of praise for his life and regret at his passing. He was praised for his "scholarly attainment," his devotion to peace until Virginia seceded from the Union, and his contributions to various charitable causes.[12] At the 1871 commencement of the College of William and Mary, the college's president noted that "the princely hospitality of Mr. William B. Harrison gave to Brandon a more than national reputation. An elegant scholar, a refined gentleman, an intelligent patriot, an earnest and devout Christian, he

William Byrd Harrison, affectionately referred to as "the squire", was remembered for his "charm... dignity...courage and high honor."

---

11. William Byrd Harrison bought Ampthill in an indenture dated October 28, 1839, for a fee of $4,000, to be paid in three annual installments. The plantation included some 1,200 acres. A deed dated September 28, 1858 passed possession of most of the plantation from him to Randolph (records of real estate transfers, Cumberland County Courthouse).
12. Biographical sketch of William Byrd Harrison in the S. Bassett French papers, VSL.

belonged to a class rapidly disappearing from Virginia. We shall not soon look on his like."[13] The respect with which he was held and the influence that he exerted on the lives of his friends and family is captured by a quotation from a grandchild. "My Father has described so vividly the life at Upper Brandon, that it is a clear picture to me. The charm, the dignity, but beyond and above all that the courage, the detestation of all that was small—the high honor of the man, so reverenced by his sons, and so affectionately referred to as 'the Squire.' "[14]

13. This statement, signed simply "A," attributes the remarks of praise to Benjamin Stoddert Ewell, the president of the college, and also notes that Harrison was the eighth generation of Harrisons to be connected with William and Mary in some capacity (Benjamin Harrison, of Wakefield, having been appointed a Visitor in 1693). This statement is found in Stanard, "Harrison of James River," pp. 188-89.
14. VMHB, XXXVII (1929), p. 80.

CHAPTER THIRTEEN

Tragedy of a System

The last third of the nineteenth century following William Byrd Harrison's death brought many other changes to the Harrison family. Harrison's widow along with her two young children, Jane and Jefferson, returned to her family home, Edgehill, in Albemarle County. There, with her three maiden sisters, all great granddaughters of Thomas Jefferson, she assisted in overseeing the Edgehill School, famous for its "Edgehill Girls."[1] Charles Shirley Harrison, one of William Byrd Harrison's sons from his first marriage, remained at Upper Brandon in the role of farm manager even after the estate was sold to his cousin. He was involved, however, in a variety of quests and controversies.[2]

In 1889 the child of a caretaker at Brandon was killed by a gunshot fired from the river, ostensibly by a man illegally hunting ducks. Deeply involved in the ensuing public uproar, Charles Shirley Harrison issued statements and letters in a war of words, alleging lack of appropriate action and footdragging by the commonwealth's attorney.[3]

1. Sarah N. Randolph, *The Domestic Life of Thomas Jefferson* (3rd ed., 1939; Albemarle County, 1871)p. 378.
2. At one point, he apparently was seeking an appointment of a highly confidential nature in the tobacco business in Richmond and sought support from both his father's longtime friend, Benjamin Stoddert Ewell, of Williamsburg, where Shirley had been a student at William and Mary (1858-59), and Hugh Blair Grigsby, confidant of both his father and his stepmother (Charles Shirley Harrison to Benjamin Stoddert Ewell, November 10, 1877, Hugh Blair Grigsby Papers, VHS).
3. *Claremont Herald*, June 3, May 7, 1889 and addendum, original in the possession of William Byrd Harrison III.

Later that year, in a lengthy letter to his brother, Harrison talked of problems with the farms, the repair to the wharf, and the possible candidacy of William Mahone for governor. Of Mahone, he wrote:

Will he be hard to beat or will we be able to bring our own whole vote against him—It is a problem that only time can solve— Are our people so poor now that many of are purchaseable—Is there not danger that they will be bought in numbers.... . Why did not the people kill him when they had an excuse to kill him at the polling place in Petersburg.[4]

That Charles Shirley Harrison took his emotions seriously, even unto death, was made clear in February 1899 at Brandon at the grave of a cousin, Isabella Ritchie Harrison. Isabella, the daughter of George Evelyn Harrison, had died on April 19, 1895, and in 1899 her body was removed to Hollywood Cemetery in Richmond.

That February, Charles Shirley Harrison left his home, which was still at Upper Brandon, and went to the empty grave. There he took out his revolver, put it against his left breast, and pulled the trigger. Although the bullet did not hit a vital spot, the discharge set his clothes afire, "and in that condition he started back for the postoffice," where a neighbor ran out and smothered the flames with snow. Harrison, however, was "in such agony that he...swallowed a bottle of laudanum" and thus expired.[5] He was fifty-seven.

None of William Byrd Harrison's children by his first wife survived much longer. Dr. George B. Harrison, the youngest, had died the previous summer at the age of fifty-three. Randolph died in September 1900 in his seventy-first year.

The age of William Byrd Harrison, and of his sons by his first marriage, and of the great plantation that they had built and nurtured, was an age of marked transition in the state and the nation. Upper Brandon in its

---

4. Charles Shirley Harrison to Randolph Harrison, August 26, 1889, ibid.
5. *Claremont Herald*, n.d., as reprinted in an unidentified paper, Bagby Family Papers, VHS. Laudanum was a form of opium popular for medicinal purposes through much of the nineteenth century.

heyday reflected both the good and the bad of the larger Virginia society. The Harrisons were kind and generous, possessed of a strong sense of loyalty, honor, and duty. They willingly made whatever sacrifices were required by circumstance to fulfill the obligations they felt were due.

Their tragedy, other than the intensely personal losses of death and suffering that seemed to strike them so often, was a tragedy shared by a system and its people, a tragedy that saw slavery as a necessity, and one that failed to recognize that no amount of kindness to a people in bondage would ever substitute for personal freedom.

In that sense, Upper Brandon, plantation on the James, was a uniquely American, uniquely southern part of history, and as such it has left us a heritage, much of it worthy of emulation, and all of it worthy of remembrance.

Sir:--We desire to call your attention to this magnificent Estate, which, as Executors, we offer for sale under the will of its late Proprietor, Wm. B. Harrison, Esq.

Well known throughout the United States, we need hardly describe it, comprising TWO FARMS *nearly equal in area, having together* SIXTEEN HUNDRED ACRES OF CHOICEST CHOCOLATE ALLUVIUM, Under the Plow, *with* SIX HUNDRED ACRES OF FOREST *in* THREE DIFFERENT NEARLY EQUAL BODIES, *within the arable surface, convenient for further division into smaller Farms.* Also, SIX HUNDRED ACRES OF MARSH LAND. *It occupies a* BEND *of the James River.*

Each Farm is supplied with durable and capacious Farm Buildings of all sorts, Granaries, Stables, Hay Houses, Managers' Houses, Quarters, &c.

The land is now under a thorough system of culture and drainage, the soil eminently suited to all grains, grasses and other products of the State; and has IN ONE YEAR, 1861, (with NO OTHER FERTILIZER than LIME AND CLOVER,) YIELDED FOR MARKET TWENTY-EIGHT THOUSAND BUSHELS OF WHEAT AND CORN. *Having bold landings at which the largest ships may load, its products are sold directly to any market of the world.*

Midway between Norfolk and Richmond, it is in daily steamboat communication with both.

The two Farms may be purchased separately, or as a unit.

The mansion and extensive grounds are peculiarly beautiful and attractive; the former a brick pile, with wings, fronting two hundred and forty feet; the latter sloping beautifully to the James River, and filled with magnificent trees and shrubbery, indigenous and exotic. For health and society, school and church privileges, this locality is not surpassed in Lower Virginia.

The river teems with fish, and the forests, fields and marshes with all the game of the section.

Parties wishing to examine the property can do so on the premises, landing from the James River Steamers at Brandon Wharf.

(SIGNED,) R. HARRISON,
          C. S. HARRISON,   } Executors.
          GEO. BYRD HARRISON,

Offer of sale of Upper Brandon properties after William Byrd Harrison's death. It was purchased by George Harrison Byrd, a nephew of William Byrd Harrison.

Epilogue

Almost immediately upon the probation of William Byrd Harrison's will, the Upper Brandon property was in effect mortgaged to one of his nephews, George Harrison Byrd (who had been born at Brandon in 1827), and another man, Samuel G. Wyman. The property ultimately passed to Byrd's son, William Byrd, and two of his siblings, Lucy Byrd Eliot and Francis Otway Byrd, the latter of whom subsequently obtained full ownership. Francis Otway Byrd retained the estate until 1948, when it was sold to Mr. and Mrs. Harry C. Thompson. The Thompsons made

February 1987 view of a refuge pond developed by James River Corporation. It has attracted an average of 3,000 wintering Canada Geese and a wide variety of ducks.

substantial structural repairs to the mansion, fully preserving its historical integrity, and resided there until it was sold in 1961 to Fred E. Watkins, of Curles Neck Farms. The house remained unoccupied for 23 years until 1984, when James River Corporation, one of the world's largest manufacturers of paper products, with headquarters in Richmond, purchased the property and undertook the restoration of the Upper Brandon mansion consistent with the occupancy of William Byrd Harrison. The company stated its intention to continue to operate the farm in the spirit of Harrison, using the latest advances in agricultural techniques, and as a demonstration farm for sound environmental practices. It also plans to establish a waterfowl refuge and generally enhance the wildlife habitat. James River is establishing a national training center for its management employees on the western reaches of the property. At the time of purchase by James River, the property consisted of 1,809.58 acres, 750 of which were under cultivation, 580 acres in marsh land, and the remainder in woods.

Appendix

The grave of William Byrd Harrison, builder of Upper Brandon, is located in the family cemetery at Brandon.

The inscription on the grave reads simply:

An eminent Agriculturist
An intelligent Patriot
An elegant Scholar
A refined Gentleman
And above all an earnest and
devoted Christian

About The Author

Robert Pendleton Hilldrup is the author of three novels and three works of nonfiction, including *Upper Brandon*. His short stories, articles, and reviews have appeared in more than sixty periodicals. He has also been visiting or adjunct faculty member in creative writing or journalism at half a dozen Virginia colleges and universities. He and his wife, Jo Ann, live in Richmond.

Index

Photo Credits

Inside front cover, drawn by Richard Stinely, Williamsburg, Virginia; pages IV & V, photo by James River Corporation; page 4, from original in Virginia Historical Society, Richmond, Virginia; page 7, from negative photostat made from original item placed in the Virginia State Library on indefinite loan by Mrs. Robert W. Daniel, Brandon, Virginia, June 30, 1966; page 10, compiled by Elizabeth Temple Johnston McRee; page 12, Fillmore Norfleet, *Saint Memin in Virginia: Portraits and Biographies*, (page 109); page 14, courtesy of William Byrd Harrison III, Richmond, Virginia; page 16, photo by James River Corporation; page 18, courtesy of The Valentine Museum, Richmond, Virginia, Cook Collection; page 20, courtesy Gordon Galusha Architects; page 21, drawings: *The American Builder's Companion*, Asher Benjamin, 1806 edition; page 21, photo: photo by James River Corporation; top page 23, courtesy of Mrs. Byrd Davenport, Richmond, Virginia, daughter of Francis Otway Byrd; bottom page 23, Cook Collection, Valentine Museum; page 24, courtesy Virginia Historical Society; page 38, courtesy of Mr. Frederick Nash Harrison Jr., Richmond, Virginia; page 42, photo by James River Corporation; page 43, courtesy of the Virginia Historical Society; page 44, photo by James River Corporation; page 46, courtesy of Virginia Historical Society; page 48, courtesy Virginia Historical Society; page 75, courtesy of Virginia Historical Society; page 82, from original at Prince George County Courthouse; page 83, *Virginia Magazine of History and Biography*, Vol. 37, 1929, (page 80); page 88, Virginia Historical Society; page 89, photo by James River Corporation.

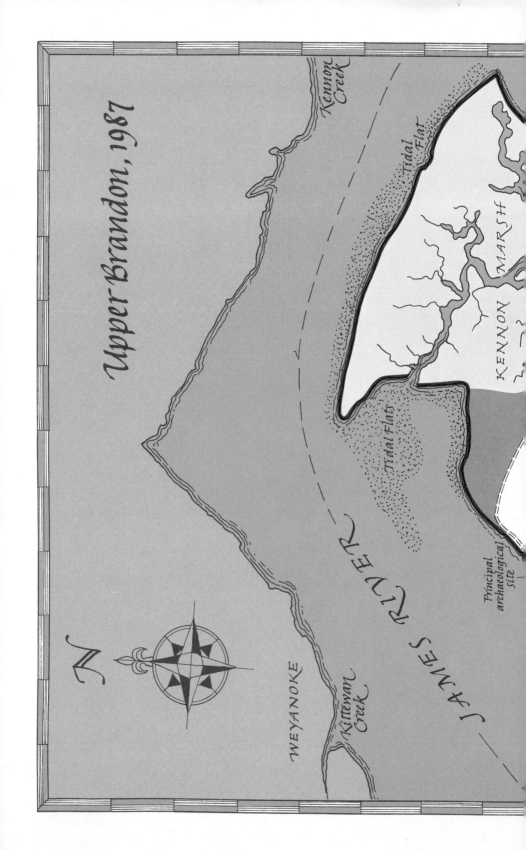

Upper Brandon, 1987

N

WEYANOKE

Kittewan Creek

JAMES RIVER

Kennon Creek

Tidal Flat

KENNON MARSH

Tidal Flats

Principal archaeological site